The Caring Classroom

by Nancy Letts

SCHOLASTIC
PROFESSIONAL BOOKS

NEW YORK • TORONTO • LONDON • AUCKLAND • SYDNEY

ACKNOWLEDGMENTS

I am pleased to be able to publicly acknowledge those who have influenced my thinking on the subject of the caring community. I am indebted to the parents, students, and teachers at the Post Road School, particularly Catherine O'Brien, for their continued support of all of my ideas.

I also want to thank Bena Kallick, Peggy McIntosh, and Judy Logan for serving as my philosophers. Their exemplary actions and original thinking have helped me to continue seeking my own truth.

My editors, Susan Shafer, Terry Cooper, and Wendy Murray have been unfailingly kind and encouraging throughout this entire project.

Thanks to the many photographers who have helped to illustrate my words: Joan Crosser, Tom Lake, Nancy Lindenauer, Lori Mollo, Mary Mysliwiec, Jean Nicastro, Maureen Rogers, Laurelle Texidore, and Alan Raymond.

Finally, I thank my family, who have taught me well what it means to care and to be cared for: Dorothy and Joe Levin, Liz and Jeff Gumbinner, and to my husband, Christopher, who has never stopped caring.

Cover design by Kathy Massaro
Cover photograph by Donnelly Marks
Interior design by Solutions by Design, Inc.

ISBN 0-590-70131-2

Contents

97058

Introduction

uring my years as a classroom teacher I often visited other teachers' classrooms. What I saw in some rooms impressed me so much that it led to the focus of my life's work and the impetus for this book.

In the successful classrooms I visited, I sensed a caring community of learners. At first, I just had an intuitive feeling about the atmosphere. I couldn't quite name what I was seeing, but I was sure it was there. Then I noticed that in some rooms, children went out of their way to help other kids. In those same classrooms children cooperated, rather than fiercely competing . What's more, in those same rooms teachers listened carefully to what kids had to say, and the teachers attempted to make curriculum meaningful for students. With time I came to understand that a caring classroom exists because a humanistic and student-centered educational philosophy is firmly in place.

Before long, I began to probe. I asked myself, "What are some of the elements in these classrooms that I can look at, so I too can make mine a caring classroom?" I began to realize that teachers in those classrooms saw what they did as part of a larger system. In fact, they looked at both their relationships with their children *and* children's relationships with one another.

In addition to looking *within* their classrooms, the teachers looked *outside* their classrooms. They said to themselves, in effect, "How can we as teachers make students' families a part of our classroom?" Of course, the teachers also looked at other people in the community, recognizing that the classroom is part of a larger arena in any town or city. I kept this information in mind.

The Purpose of This Book

After many years of teaching, I became an educational consultant, evaluator, and speaker. I was guided by a desire to work with schools across the country who were examining their assumptions about teaching and learning. To this day, whichever district I visit, I make sure that I have opportunities to watch teachers and students in action. I want to see—and confirm to myself—why some classrooms seem to run all by themselves. Over time, I have learned a number of qualities about caring classrooms and how they become that way. The purpose of this book, then, is to share with you what I have learned over the years about how a caring classroom is formed, and enriched over time. No matter how successful our teaching is, we can build on our successes by keeping in mind a picture of what caring education should be.

Book's Structure

The following chapters provide a framework for teaching and learning in the caring classroom. I am not trying to prescribe a formula or a recipe for success; caring is not formulaic. We cannot *touch* care or *see* it in conventional ways. It requires, first of all, a thoughtful attention to ideas and I've tried to focus on these ideas in this book.

Chapter one sets the tone for thinking about the ideas of caring in an interconnected system. There is an impact on each part of that system, and it has an impact on every other part. The student is part of her classroom, which is connected to the larger school, which is connected to the home, which is connected to the immediate community, which is connected to the larger world, which is connected to the student.

Chapter two gives the reader an opportunity to "be there" on the first day of school. It's during those first days and weeks that the tone of the caring community is established, but most of us never have the opportunity to focus on those decisive moments.

Chapter three describes how to bring caring into your curriculum, because it is impossible to develop meaningful curriculum without thinking of the underlying pedagogy. The chapter describes curricula that are embedded in the values of caring, not ones that are added on to an already hectic schedule.

Chapter four discusses dialogue as an essential tool in the caring classroom. Skills and behaviors can be deliberately taught through dialogue. I also show how those skills can be transferred to other areas of learning.

Chapter five, "Managing the Caring Classroom", is the most problematic for me. Ideally, a classroom that is constructed on the values of care should not need to be "managed." The reality, however, is that we still have a way to go, therefore, I have presented ideas that other teachers are using successfully in their classrooms. I caution against a one-size-fits-all approach and hope that the reader will see managing behavior in its larger context.

Chapter six focuses on the close of the school year. The emphasis is on celebrating our successes and on learning to value the best of what we do. Reflection and goal setting are the signs of a thoughtful practitioner. We must build time for thinking into every school day. Otherwise, why would we ask our students to do what we are not prepared to do?

CHAPTER ONE

Why Care About Caring?

ne spring some years ago, when I left Patty Dempsey's first grade class, I was certain that I had just witnessed a wonderful example of a caring classroom in action. Patty and her students sat in a circle on the floor, in a corner of the room that they used for class talk. Patty asked the children if anyone had a problem that they needed help with.

Mary Ellen said: "Sometimes when I'm on the bus, a mean kid comes up to me. When I have to get off at my stop he buckles up the belts across, and then I can't get out. Does anyone have a suggestion?" She saw Peter's hand and called on him.

"You could tell him not to do it, and if he won't stop then you could tell the bus driver."

"I'll give it a try."

David was next. "I have a problem. I don't like it when I go outside sometimes in the spring and people gang up on me. I don't know what to do."

"You could say, 'Would you please stop bothering me?' Or you could play by your-self for a while," Ross suggested.

"I'll try. Adam, do you have a solution to my problem?"

"You could say to them, 'How would you like it if I did that to you?'"

"That might work. Sandy?"

"You could say to them, 'Please stay out of my personal space.'"

Throughout the discussion, Patty listened carefully. She never spoke, and the students did not seek her advice. She only spoke when it was time for class talk to be over: "Could you let us know the next time we have our class talk if any of these suggestions have helped you?" In unison the first graders said, "sure," and returned to their desks.

I sat alone on the rug after everyone left. I marveled at this scene. Patty and her students made it all look so easy, but I knew that they had to learn how to listen care-fully and how to respond to one another with thoughtfulness.

What Does It Mean to Care?

There was no doubt that Patty Dempsey's first graders cared about the prob-lems their friends described. It was also evident that Patty was concerned, too. She gave them time to talk about serious problems. She also demonstrated which tools—words, behaviors, and attitudes—show compassion. By accepting with-out judgment the advice they gave to one another she attributed the best possible motives to each child's efforts.

After I first met with Patty I began looking for other examples of caring classrooms. I was anxious to determine what qualities these communities of learners shared.

I noticed, first, that in a caring classroom:

❋ A trusting relationship exists between the teacher and each student *and* between student and student.

❋ Shows positive relations.

❋ There is a sense of self-control among individual members as well as a feeling of responsibility to the group.

Fifth-graders at Searington school prepare to plant impatiens in their school garden. Learning to care for local environments is an essential part of their curriculum.

The Caring Classroom and the Student

A caring classroom is a highly personalized environment. For better or worse, a student cannot hide. The very act of being visible all the time provides the opportunity for relationships to develop and to become more central to the heart of the learning experience. Students who are respected and attended to are more willing to trust the teacher. Students who feel like valued members of a community work harder to see that the community succeeds. The greater the responsibility a student feels toward the group the more that student will work toward maintaining the norms of behavior that are accepted by that group.

> **QUESTIONS THAT MEMBERS OF A CARING COMMUNITY ASK:**
>
> 1. *What kind of person do I want to be?*
> 2. *What do I want others to think of me?*
> 3. *What kind of classroom, school, and community do I want?*

Start-of-School Unit on Names

One way you might encourage students to develop positive relationships with each other is to begin the year by confirming the importance of each student's name. Judi Sparken, a teacher in Indiana, begins by distributing several poems and short pieces of prose to her fifth graders. These might include the short story "No Name Woman" by Maxine Hong Kingston, "My Name" by Sandra Cisneros, "If I Had Been Called Sabrina," a poem by Marge Piercy, or "Zami: A New Spelling of My Name," by Audre Lorde. Students read these short pieces as powerful examples of ways we are named or ways that we name ourselves.

SLIPPERY

The six month child
Fresh from the tub
Wriggles in our hands.
This is our fish child.
Give her a nickname: Slippery
—Carl Sandburg

Students then introduce themselves to a partner by sharing the story of their own names. Resources that provide further clues to the source of a child's name are available in the classroom: what-to-name-the-baby books, stories of Greek and African mythology, dictionaries, and books on etymology.

Judi's fifth graders warmed to this introduction of one another. Iris found out that she was named for the Greek goddess of the rainbow. Seroka told how her mother simply loved the sound of the word. Several boys told how they were named for their fathers. "Is there a special responsibility that you feel, being named for your father?" Judi asked, and the class began a spirited discussion of the importance of names.

By the end of the unit each student learned the correct spelling and pronunciation of every other name in her class. Students had engaged in sustained written and oral research. They read for comprehension. They practiced skills of communication. They wrote to detail their research. They also wrote in journals to reflect on their experiences.

"I never used to like my name, because the kids always made fun of it . But now I'm proud of it." (Allison)

"I didn't really know the names of all of the other kids in the room before we did this." (Tamara)

"I think we're going to have a good time in class this year. The kids seem nicer and friendlier in fifth grade. I don't exactly know why but I'm glad anyway." (Jeremy)

CHILDREN WHO CARE:

1. *Respect themselves.*
2. *Feel valued by other members of the class.*
3. *Share a sense of belonging to something larger than themselves.*
4. *Have an opportunity to practice the skills and behaviors that engender a caring environment.*

The Caring Classroom and the Teacher

Most of us are teachers because we honestly care about kids, but teaching the ethic of care seems to have lost its place in the curriculum. Relationships—the heart of the caring classroom—nurture and inspire the teacher as well as the student. From where else do we get our strength if not from the student?

Too often, teaching goes in one direction: From us to them. When we write objectives or design assessments we are interested in improving student achievement and in expanding students' knowledge. A caring classroom community, on the other hand, allows learning to flow in both directions. Teachers and students can explore together the respect for one another that is essential to sustaining group life.

An Openness to Ideas

Marilyn Edwards, a third-grade teacher in a small school in the northeast, provides us with a good example of this democratic view of living, teaching, and learning. One March, she began to plan for her unit for Women's History Month. In the past she would have written curriculum, gathered resources from the library and taught the unit. This time, however, she decided to call some parents first.

"Hi, Mrs. Jackson. This is Marilyn Edwards," she said. "Could you give me some advice? I'd like your help in planning my next unit. I want my students to learn more about women from all walks of life and from the many groups that make up our town. Are there specific things that you think would be useful for kids to know? Are there women that you think should be included in our study?"

When Marilyn asked for support and information from Mrs. Jackson and other mothers of her students, she fortified her relationship not only to the parents but to their children as well. Her connection to the lives of the mothers and her eagerness to include their knowledge and experience in classroom learning is a powerful act of caring. She was not asking Mrs. Jackson to write her curriculum—she was inviting them to enrich it. She was signaling to them that she valued them.

The Caring Classroom, Principals, and Other Administrators

Instructional leaders who examine the culture of their schools—that is, the rituals, stories, and symbols that exemplify the school community—have an opportunity to transform those rituals into positive, affirming ones that model a larger caring community. Many rituals in our schools rely on winning and losing. Award ceremonies, spelling bees, and traditional sports teams describe most school cultures. With careful planning we can help schools focus instead on becoming places where relationship and community are central.

Welcome to the Smith Street School

One morning I arrived at the Smith Street School early. As I walked through the hallway, I heard singing. I followed the music and soon was standing in the back of the gymnasium/auditorium. The whole school was there, and the air was alive with wonderful sound. First through fifth graders sat on the floor in rows singing and clapping to "This Land Is My Land."About ten parents stood in the back with me. When the singing stopped several second graders took turns at the microphone to read reports they had written. Some of them read fluently and with feeling, others spoke in more halting voices, stopping to sound words out or to ask for help from the teacher.

What impressed me most was the audience. No one whispered, giggled, or disparaged the readers. There was a deliberate attempt on the part of the audience to support and to celebrate the efforts of these second graders.

The second part of the program was even more special. Each guest or visitor who was seated in the back was introduced by the student who invited them. The first child to speak into the microphone was six-year-old Jamal. "I would like to introduce you to my grandmother, Mrs. Clarese White. When Mrs. White appeared in the front of the room, the students applauded. Mrs. White was presented with a certificate of appreciation and was escorted back to her place by Jamal. Each guest was honored just like Mrs. White. The students in the audience remained attentive throughout.

Finally the principal walked to the microphone. He told the students that in the evening, twenty-two high school students would be honored for community service. "I'm going to read the names of all of these students. If any one of them is a relative of yours, please stand. You see, if any one in your family does something honorable it brings honor to all members of your family and to all parts of our school community." Five students stood and received enthusiastic applause.

Karen Siris is the assistant principal of the Smith Street School. She and a group of teachers had organized the morning program. Every morning for twenty minutes the entire school assembles. Each grade level is responsible for organizing the morning program for a month. The format is the same each day: The students sing songs (which are written on large chart paper and are played on a cassette recorder), watch short skits or presentations, and honor the guests who are in the audience.

The instructional leaders at the Smith Street School have re-created a ritual around relationships and connectedness that communities feel for their members. The morning program at the Smith Street School left me with little doubt that caring on a schoolwide level can be taught, learned, and celebrated.

The Caring Classroom and Parents

Most teachers understand how integral schools are to the moral development of children. This comes at a time when teachers and parents seem locked in tense discussions about just what the proper role of schools should be. Few would disagree that schools, in order to be most effective, need the backing of parents. And parents need the same support from schools.

Families are quick to pick up on the effects of a positive school culture. Parents whose children are members of caring classrooms have reported to me the changes they see at home with comments like these:

> "Jason has stopped picking on his younger brother. He keeps trying to compromise with Kyle, to find things that they can do together. We've noticed that Jason has begun using some of the phrases that you use in school, and we think that what you are doing is beginning to have an effect at home. "

> "Katherine doesn't complain any more that things aren't fair in school."

> "What are you doing in your classroom? Peter's been feeding the dog every morning. All by himself. I only had to remind him once—last Wednesday—and that was because he was running late."

Know Your Students Well

A child whose teacher and parents support one another because they are both committed to the same social and academic goals is more likely to understand and act on those goals. One evening my phone rang. It was Jim Eisenberg, a parent of a student I taught several years ago. Bekka was in my fifth grade class the year we put on a review for Women's History Month. I recall Bekka telling the story about the female elephant who was queen of the jungle. Bekka's demeanor that day was far from the reserved young lady I usually saw in class. She was bold when she became that elephant. She stood alone on the stage with her hands on her hips and her legs askew, and, with an attitude that would make even the most ferocious lion keep his distance, Rebecca *roared* the punch line.

I spent more time with Bekka after that, helping her to find strong, personal connections in other areas of the curriculum. When we studied Greek mythology I helped her find many versions of stories about Athena and Diana, godesses who used their own strength to find success. I also encouraged her to find ways to connect math, her least favorite subject, with music, art, and poetry, subjects close to her heart. Jim's phone call brought those memories home. "I've been meaning to call you for awhile now. I want you to know how important you were to Bekka's development. Many of Bekka's friends have become more and more quiet in the classroom or—worse—are 'dumbing themselves down' so that they won't stand out. Your taking the time to know her and to help her in the fifth grade has helped her to stand up for herself in the eighth grade. She's taught us to really listen to her when she talks and to take her seriously—just as you did. We all want to thank you."

> **WHEN WORKING WITH PARENTS, KEEP IN MIND:**
>
> ❈ *Parents also want the best for their children.*
>
> ❈ *Learn to value the hopes and the goals that parents express for their children.*
>
> ❈ *Make your actions and your words convey to parents that you recognize their child as an individual.*

The Caring Classroom and the Larger Community

If being a member of a caring classroom benefits the student and extends to the family, can we assume that members of caring classrooms are assets to the local communities as well? The answer is often "yes" when teachers extend the notion of care beyond their classrooms. Teachers who develop a knowledge of local resources can use this information profitably to increase their students' skills and

A third grader shares a book she has written with a member of the Elder Care Community in Westwood, New Jersey.

talents. When we know more about how the community can become available to students, we can enlarge our own awareness of the community's resources to enrich curriculum and instruction.

Environmental Study Benefits All

Jackson Edwards was ready to engage community resources in new ways as he began a unit on the environment. He helped his fourth grade students list every environmental problem they could think of: a dying creek on the outskirts of town, a beach with the flotsam and jetsam of the past winter, dirty sidewalks in the business district, a vacant lot littered with debris, potholes, and

"What the best and wisest parent wants for his own child, that must the community want for all its children."
—John Dewey

cracks in the roads and sidewalks. Next Jackson led them through brainstorming exercises to name the agencies and organizations in the town who might provide help. They were abetted by the telephone directory and a League of Women Voters list of town leaders and agencies. They tried to match the agencies with the environmental problems named on the lists. Their initial plan was to write letters to the agencies asking each for information on the environmental work in which they were presently engaged.

Students learn about fish morphology with Christopher Letts, a naturalist and Hudson River Educator. Mentors like Christopher help to expand students' vision of the world.

JACKSON EDWARDS AND A GRADE FOUR PLAN

1. *Create Partnership Teams that include parents, students, and community members.*
2. *Define the problem for each team to work on and devise a plan for implementing that work. This work would not be the sole responsibility of the students; instead, each member of the partnership would share in the effort.*
3. *Write letters to the newspaper and to town officials asking for help.*
4. *Document progress with charts, drawings, photographs, and journals.*
5. *Meet as a class each Friday afternoon from 2:00–3:00 to talk about the progress or concerns of each partnership team and to decide what next steps should be taken.*

When they met with only limited success in getting agencies to respond they decided to ask the agencies how they, the fourth graders, might help. This time they received practical advice and examples. Using that information from the responses Jackson helped the students devise an action plan.

Jackson was fairly expansive in his notion of the caring community. He helped his students understand that it includes all the strengths and talents found in any neighborhood.

FIVE WAYS FOR STUDENTS TO BUILD CARING LOCAL COMMUNITIES

1. *Gather information on community activities that link to learning skills and talents, such as after school or summer programs for students.*
2. *Work with the PTA or PTO to provide programs in the community that strengthen family practices, such as Saturday trips to a local art museum or zoo.*
3. *Inaugurate service projects through the local civic, counseling, cultural, health, and recreation organizations, as well as through business associations.*
4. *Provide services to senior citizens by students and/or their families*
5. *Stay in touch with alumni who can provide school or classroom programs.*

What Will a Caring Classroom Accomplish?

For six months fifth graders and kindergartners at the Ralph M. Maughm School in New Jersey team up. They often eat lunch together, do special projects together, and share recess time. Here are their evaluations of their partnership at midyear :

Fifth Graders Comment:

"We were shy at first but now we are good friends." (Alex)

"The fifth graders have grown in patience, especially when we are outside with the kindergartners at lunchtime." (Lindsay)

"The fifths realize they were once very young like the kindergartners and felt like they do." (Jordan)

"The partnerships are more than just doing projects together. They are about becoming good friends."(Ben)

"In the beginning of the year, we did not have a lot to talk about but now we have a lot to share with each other." (Megan)

Kindergartners Comment:

"As the year has passed we have become good friends with all the fifth graders." (Ada)

"Sometimes when kindergartners hang out with their partners, it makes them feel special." (Ariel)

"Good friends make good friendships." (Dominque)

"Good times can never end with your partner." (Brian)

"My partner has a good idea and I think that is special." (Roman)

Elements of a Caring Classroom

Let's examine these components to see what has been learned about being part of a caring community of learners.

Relationships Are the Priority

Many of the students understand the high value of relationships. The two teachers involved in this partnership plan their curriculum carefully. Many of the cooperative activities are created so that both age groups have something to contribute. Sometimes it's only the fifth graders who do the teaching; just as often, it's the kindergartners.

Teachers Model Caring Actions

Several of the students refer to *then and now*. "We used to be. . . but now we. . ." During the year both teachers used the feedback from each partnership and their own observations of the experience to plan their next time together. When several of the children complained about not being listened to, the teachers role-played effective ways to be active listeners. They speak with each other in front of the class so that students could hear thoughtful dialogue.

Modeling behaviors—respecting another's opinions, encouraging and supporting each others' ideas, and accepting without judging—make implicit behaviors visible to all students. When teachers model words and the body language that supports the words, they help students see the connection between what we say and how we act. It is through the consistency of our words and our actions that the caring classroom takes shape.

Teachers Encourage Empathy

We see, for example, that Jordan has learned to be more empathetic. Jordan tells us that he (and the other fifths) remembers what it was like to be five years old. He tells us that he knows what it is like to put one's self in another's place.

What Jordan means, we presume, is that by remembering himself as a kindergartner he will not expect the younger kids to think or behave like ten year olds. He will choose activities and learning experiences that are based on what he observes, instead of what satisfies his own needs.

WHAT CAN WE DO TO BUILD A CARING CLASSROOM?

1. *Continually Draw Connections Between Principles and Actions.* Teach children the underlying principles that guide the caring classroom. Help them make the connection between the principles and their manifestation. Ask them, "What does respect look like? What does it sound like?"

2. *Establish Expectations.* Allow time to practice the procedures that contribute to a caring classroom. Name the social behaviors you want to target. Model, demonstrate, role-play. Let kids know you expect much of them and then let them know how valuable their prosocial behavior is to the well-being of the classroom community.

3. *Create Meaningful Curricula.* Help children "find" themselves in the curriculum. If we can build curricula that are fluid, evolving, and engaging we will provide both a window and a mirror for all students. We will increase their involvement with learning and provide a personal means to reinforce the social values that support a caring classroom.

4. *Show Respect.* Let children know that they are valued and respected members of the classroom.

5. *Let Children Make Choices.* Kids learn to become responsible by being given responsibility. In fact, students who are able to exercise self-determination have a higher degree of self-confidence. Give them lots of opportunities to make choices. Help them learn from their successes as well as from their mistakes and to plan for future behavior.

What Will I Expect to See in a Caring Classroom?

Participatory Decision Making

Patty Dempsey told me a story about her first graders:

"The other morning a group of children in my class huddled around a book called *Fix It*. Someone read the first page: 'But Emma had a big problem.' Amanda's head snapped up and a big smile spread across her face. 'Miss Dempsey,' she began, 'Emma should come to our class talk. We would help her solve her problem!'"

"My class is solving problems left and right," Dempsey continued. "I wish you could be a fly on the wall and listen to them exploring their options and settling disputes. While the number of conflicts that arises is no less than in previous years, the number of times my intervention is necessary is marginal in comparison."

Class Meetings

In Patty Dempsey's first grade class or Diane Celatano's fifth grade one flight up, students are involved in a variation of the class meeting. During each meeting there are examples of students practicing caring behavior. You would notice:

* ***The Meetings Are Held Daily.*** Patty begins hers first thing in the morning so that the students can talk about the day before them; Diane finds after lunch a better time to meet. Problems sometimes arise during recess so the fifth graders decided that settling them directly from the playground is more beneficial. Both teachers agree on the need to call meetings any time if the need arises.

* ***Students Set the Agenda.*** The teachers add to the list, but the kids decide what is necessary to talk about.

* ***Prosocial Skills Are in Evidence.*** Students wait for one person to stop speaking before they take their turn. They decide how to be fair in giving everyone a turn.

* ***Students Are Central to Giving Advice or Suggesting Alternatives to Problems.*** The teacher only intervenes when the students ask for it or if she feels that her suggestions would be a valuable addition.

* ***The class meeting*** lasts about twenty minutes. Longer than that? Kids begin to get fidgety.

Class meetings are an example of Lawrence Kohlberg's notion of the "just community." Their aim is to help students learn to make moral decisions. The just community relies on participatory decision making, focusing on fairness and justice. Every student is encouraged to contribute. Patty Dempsey and Diane Celatano want their students to think about answering "What is best for the good of the group?" and not "What is best for me?"

Making Classroom Procedures Run Smoothly

A substitute teacher once confided to me how hard it was to work in different classrooms every day, "except for Billie DeJanero's class," she said. "I'd like to bottle what that woman does. Her students act the same for me as they do for her."

IT'S NOT MAGIC BUT MODELING

Billie DeJanero spent time and effort teaching her students to take responsibility for their own classroom. If you were to visit her third grade class when the substitute was there, here's what you might see:

❀ *Students move quietly from whole class discussions to small-group work. They know where the materials are kept for their ongoing projects. They get what they need from the shelves and the baskets located around their learning centers.*

❀ *Every student is responsible for some caretaking activity that helps to make the classroom run smoothly and efficiently. Kids are paper monitors, plant waterers, rabbit feeders, board washers, recyclers, cubby straighteners. Everyone seems to take pride in his or her role and knows what is necessary to do the job well.*

❀ *Kids speak kindly. Words like please and thank you are commonplace.*

❀ *Students have a vocabulary for mediating disputes. Students ask for what they want instead of blaming others for not giving it.*

❀ *Students Know How to Compromise. Listen too for evidence of compromise in this third grade class: "What if I use the lefty scissors until ten-twenty and then you use it until we go to phys ed?"*

Home and Community Involvement

Primary School Haven

Nonny Hagen's primary school sits in the center of an urban area in the midwest. The building is surrounded by what most would consider decay: vacant factories, littered lots, and boarded-up row houses. But there is no mistaking the refuge Nonny has created in her red brick building. At lunchtime every room in the school is lit up with the energy of vibrant voices and purposeful work. In a makeshift art room, several students work with an art teacher and a parent on face masks they'll use in a program celebrating African tribal dances.

In the auditorium, two men—barbers by profession—are teaching a group of students the words to an aria. They are singing in Italian. Nobody in the school speaks Italian, but that doesn't deter either the men or their six students. The kids are trying to learn the music to sing in an upcoming talent show. It was their idea to have the show and their idea to invite the barbers to teach them opera. One man stands next to the turntable, stopping the music to make a point. The other repeats the words of the song and sings along with the tenor on the record. After awhile the kids begin to sing a refrain with the older men. The children's faces are expressions of intense concentration.

REMEMBER: THIS IS WHAT'S INVOLVED IN SETTING UP THE CARING CLASSROOM

❀ *Modeling by the teacher of desirable ways of interacting.*

❀ *Dialogue which values the speaker as well as what is spoken.*

❀ *Practice for children in order to internalize the skills and behaviors.*

❀ *Confirmation of children's best efforts.*

We know that they'll learn the music in time for the show.
Here are some other views of Nonny Hagen's school:

1. *Adult Learning.* Courses for parents including literacy classes, GED courses, and training for teacher assistants. These courses emphasize the same skills and prosocial behaviors for creating caring classrooms that are taught to students. Teachers of adults show how families can establish environments to support children *at home*.

2. *Groups Put Heads Together.* A parent, teacher, and translator meet about the ways the school and the family can support a bilingual child.

3. *Involved Parents.* Parents look through the weekly folder of work that their children take home each Friday. Some parents are reading comments from the students or their teachers. Others are writing their own comments or questions about the work.

4. *Garden Activities.* Three staff members from a local hardware store plant bulbs with a group of second graders. They have already worked together to build birdhouses, make a bench, and paint a sign announcing THE GARDEN FOR ALL GOD'S THINGS.

5. *Warmth Shown.* One mother sits in Nonny's office sorting old clothes and mittens that will be set aside in boxes and kept for kids who need an extra set of something or other.

6. *Portfolios.* Addie Locasio, who has been trained as the school's video maker, interviews a second grader for her reading portfolio. She asks each question as if the seven year old were being interviewed for a television talk show:

   "What's your favorite kind of book, darling?"

   "Why do you suppose people read?"

   "What is your reading goal for next year?"

   "How about picking a book and reading a page for me?"

Addie participates in a twice-a-year effort to document each child's literacy performance. By the time they graduate from fifth grade, each child will have a record of her progress. If Addie can't make it, she'll call upon the several other adults she's taught to do the job.

7. *Large Parent Presence.* PTA and PTO meetings are attended by better than 50 percent of the parent body. Family homework nights are a big success. Parents and their children solve math problems together or write poetry in two voices. Music nights are popular. Parents and other community members are encouraged to participate in talent nights. Baby-sitting and transportation are always provided.

8. *Overnight Trip.* Nonny Hagen worked with a local environmental educator to have parents and kids sleep out one night in the woods of the nature center. After a full day of hiking, exploring, bonfires, and marshmallows, the class of third graders and the parents who attended slept soundly in the great outdoors. On the bulletin board to the left of the entrance are the photographs of that overnight trip. See the smiles on everyone's faces. They'll return next year, I'll bet.

These parents and this community knows that they are cared for. In return, they lavish care on their school and on the children in the school.

HOW TO INVOLVE THE FAMILY AND COMMUNITY

❊ *Establish Neighborhood Patrols.* Ask school officials to set up neighborhood watch patrols to ensure that all of the children will get to school and home again safely.

❊ *Tape Events.* Tape all workshops and exhibitions so that kids can watch them or listen to them at home with the family.

❊ *Conduct Oral History Events.* Develop an oral history project to teach students about history. Interview community members who might bear witness to past events and who can make history come alive.

❊ *Translate Special Works.* Ask bilingual children to translate stories, poems, or songs from English into their native language and to read the translated works to their parents. This way non-English-speaking parents can enjoy the stories too.

❊ *Meet Outside School.* From time to time, hold PTA or PTO meetings away from school. Experiment with neighborhood community centers, meeting rooms in apartment houses, even restaurants.

❊ *Invite Senior Citizens on Trips.* In New York, one fourth grade visits Ellis Island every year to culminate their unit on immigration. Last year they took along a group of seniors from a local nursing home.

Teach Caring in Every Exchange

Teaching is filled with many opportunities to show that we care. In every relationship members decide how they want to respond to each other. We have a choice. If we are talking to another person and a student interrupts, we can say, "Oh, I'll bet you forgot to wait your turn." Or we can say, "How many times do I have to tell you to wait your turn?" In a caring classroom we begin by attributing to the student the best motives for her actions. We reinforce those behaviors by acting in a consistent manner with our words. We provide lots of opportunities for students to practice what they see demonstrated.

Why care about caring? Because in order to be cared for we must learn how to care for others. Each is dependent on the other. It is in the best interest of a participatory democracy to maintain and deepen the relationships that embody caring.

Action Plan: What Can I Do Today?

Keep a journal in which you observe one to three students in your class. If you choose a few students on whom to focus it will be easier to follow their efforts.

- ✻ Write for no more than fifteen minutes, or less, at the end of each day.

- ✻ Focus on one skill. What action did you notice or observe that showed respect, responsibility, kindness, or empathy?

- ✻ What did the student say or do to inform you of his response to your modeling, demonstrating, or dialogue?

CHAPTER TWO

The First Month of School

T he first time I visited the Winthrop School I knew that I was in a special place. I could sense the tone. It was the end of the day and dismissal had begun. Students and teachers stood together in several small groups on the patches of grass that surround the driveway. These were the children who were waiting to be picked up by family members. They did not seem to be arranged by grade, yet each child was accounted for. Some were in line to get on to the school buses and others were talking. Adults and children interacted comfortably—evidence of mutual respect. I overheard bits of their conversation:

"Willy, did you remember the permission slip for field day? Do you think your mother will be able to come to see you run the one-k? Do you want me to call and remind her?"

"Didn't we have a great time at the river today? Do you think the animals we collected will live happily together in our tank?"

"Now, don't forget; what's the first thing you're going to do when you get home this afternoon?"

The Winthrop School is located in a transitional neighborhood that continues to feel the effects of many long-time industries closing down. Some middle-class parents have either moved from the community or have placed their children in private schools. Yet the Winthrop School continues to serve children with a passion and a commitment to the belief that all children can learn. Laurelle Texidore, the principal, and the faculty at Winthrop have paid careful attention to creating a tone of decency, both formally and informally. The faculty recognize their responsibility not only to the students and to the community but also to one another. Laurelle tells me that her teachers "walk their talk."

A poster with this poem greets all who enter the Winthrop School:

EXCELLENCE CAN BE ATTAINED IF YOU...
Care more than others think is wise.
Risk more than others think is safe.
Dream more than others think is practical.
Expect more than others think is possible.
—Author Unknown

A Tone of Decency for All School Members

The way each member of a school community behaves toward one another sets a tone that has a powerful effect on what students learn. In each of the public spaces in our schools—classrooms, hallways, main offices, lunchrooms, playgrounds, school bus lines—students see and hear behavior that allows them to construct meaning about the culture of their school community.

Which of the following qualities does your school community exhibit?

- Students and teachers speak to one another with kindness and respect.

- The hallways are clean and filled with examples of student work.

- Student displays are labeled so that visitors know what they are looking at and how it fits into the curriculum.

- Nonnegotiable rules for students and faculty are fair and consistently enforced. Negotiable rules are created as part of a participatory democracy.

- Intellectual rigor is respected and honored.

The First Morning:
The Formation of a Community

"Last year, right after lunch on the first day of school, a mother walked into my classroom with her son. Everett didn't come to school that morning because his mother didn't think it was very important." Minty O'Brien is describing an incident that forced her to realize that by the first afternoon of the first day her class had already become a community. "Because Everett arrived in class a few hours after the other children, he became 'the new kid' when he showed up that afternoon. That's how powerful the morning's learning experience is for my students."

Minty has taught every grade in her K-5 school. "I want to know where they've been and where they're going!" she tells me. Her procedure for the first morning of the first day is the same—with minor variations—no matter what grade she's teaching. She sets a tone of respect and decency that gives students structure and comfort. She establishes routines with her students. "When you assume the best motives for your students—and when they know what it is they are supposed to do—you can almost see the anxiety of that first morning vanish."

How Minty O'Brien Gets Her Students Off To The Right Start

1. *She Greets Children Warmly.* "You can sit wherever you want to right now." Minty greets each student at they enter the classroom. She modulates her voice to maintain a soft and relaxed tone. "Later I'm going to change the seats." Minty reserves the right to place children in seating patterns, but she makes that information clear to the class right away.

2. *She Uses Nonverbal Clues.* "You are able to sit longer and to pay attention if you center your body in your seat."

   After the children are settled at their desks Minty begins teaching them nonverbal signals that she uses with consistency throughout the year.

   She models how to sit "comfortable and tall"—which eventually becomes "comfortably tall" as the year progresses. "If you need to be reminded to sit comfortable and tall I will *tap my shoulder*." She does, and every child sits up. Nonverbal clues are a respectful way to remind students about procedures they might have forgotten. Such signals diminish the teacher's voice as an enforcer and make for a much more peaceful environment.

   Moving her chair is another nonverbal signal that Minty repeats daily. "When you see me pull my chair over to the side of the room and sit down, that should be a signal for you to come up and sit down. Please cross your arms in front of you and place your whole body so that you can see me." When the children are seated "comfortably tall" Minty reads them *Chicka Chicka Boom Boom* (by Bill Martin, Jr., and John Archambault, illustrated by Lois Ehlert) or another story or poem that requires choral reading or responses from the class. "Chick-A-Boom/Chick-A-Boom/Chick-A-Boom Boom Boom. . ." they repeat with obvious delight.

3. ***She Allows for Differences in Learning Styles and Pace.*** "You may go back to your seat and write a story. Or you may stay on the rug and ask me a question." Minty begins to model the routine that will follow their coming together. Beginning the next day she will use this time to teach a mini-lesson in the writing process and introduce a concept in math. Those who have no questions are free to return to their seats and work on the open-ended problems in writing or math. Those who have questions remain on the rug.

    This procedure allows for differences in learning. Students who are able to move ahead by themselves are free to begin; they are not held up with questions that have little meaning for them. Those who need more attention learn to ask the questions that will help Minty guide their learning.

4. ***She Establishes Herself as the Authority.*** When many children appear to have finished their first assignment Minty says to the class, "See if you can find a space in the room where you can stand without touching the furniture or one another. Make sure you have room to move your arms." Minty models for the class. Soon they are all stationed around the classroom. "Make sure you can all see my eyes." This time she establishes herself as the authority.

5. ***She Introduces a Fun Activity.*** When every eye is on her she picks up a large rag doll. "I'd like to introduce you to my friend, Raggedy Ann."

RAGGEDY ANN IS MY BEST FRIEND
Raggedy Ann is my best friend
She's so relaxed
Just watch her bend
First from the waist
Then from the knee
Her arms are swinging
Oh, so free
Her head rolls around
Like a rubber ball
She hasn't any bones at all
But Raggedy Ann
Can stand up tall.

—Author Unknown

Minty taps her shoulder, reminding the class to stand tall. "Listen to the poem and watch Raggedy." She twists and turns the doll, letting it flop around. She moves her limbs and body in a loose and easy way. She's obviously enjoying herself as she repeats the poem. "Now it's your turn," she tells the students. Even the most shy have now joined in. Everyone loves being silly.

6. *Good Posture Indicates Respect.* "Do you remember how you were supposed to sit? Can you return to your seats and show me?" Minty has brought the procedures full circle. She tries to seat the doll, but Raggedy slumps all over herself. "Why can't the doll sit 'beautiful and tall'?"

The children offer several reasons. Minty focuses on two: It doesn't have a brain. It has no bones. Minty uses this discussion to reinforce the ideas that we're different from Raggedy Ann, because humans use a brain to think and because they have a structure in their bodies that support good posture.

It's time for lunch. Minty has used this first morning in a carefully sequenced way to introduce the experience of being a member of a caring community. She has also prepared students for their afternoon science lesson on the human body! As the weeks continue she will add additional procedures. Each will be taught deliberately through modeling, demonstration, practice, and validation.

MINTY O'BRIEN'S "FIRST MORNING" PRINCIPLES

- *A quiet voice sets a calming tone.*
- *Nonverbal signals are kinder and less threatening than verbal ones.*
- *Reminders can be sandwiched between slices of praise.*
- *We can teach about personal boundaries and classroom procedures through continued modeling and demonstration.*
- *Good posture and eye contact indicate respect for the speaker.*

Other Procedures to Practice During the First Weeks of School

- Bathroom routines.
- Moving to partner or group work.
- Getting paper or other materials to begin a task.
- Walking through the halls.
- Solving a problem without first asking the teacher for help.
- Caring for pets, plants, and materials in the classroom.
- Putting books and materials away after they have been used.

The Second Week: Reinforcement

1. ***Create Connections Through Writing Projects.*** Tape large sheets of paper to the walls around the room. Head each one with sentence starters such as THE BEST BOOK I READ THIS SUMMER WAS...MY FAVORITE SUBJECT IN SCHOOL IS...THE FARTHEST PLACE I HAVE TRAVELED IS...MY FAVORITE HOLIDAY IS...THE NICEST THING ANYONE EVER SAID ABOUT ME WAS...

   Give students a crayon or marker as they enter the classroom. Ask them to circle the room and complete the sentences on each sheet. Encourage children to sign their names to their responses.

   When they have completed the task, walk around the room, commenting on what you've noticed: the similarities of the responses, the uniqueness of some, the connections you see.

2. ***Give Your Class a Name.*** Teach children how to build consensus by deciding on a name, logo, or symbol for the class. Demonstrate how consensus building moves beyond winning or losing. "Can you live with this name for a period of time?" (at which time you would return to see whether the name was still suitable) or "What would it take for you to feel comfortable with the decision?" are questions that can unblock a discussion when it gets stuck.

   Students might want to put their class name or logo on stationery, T-shirts, or banners that decorate the room.

3. ***Begin a Class Book.*** Ask the students, "How might we show and tell about our class this year?" You might begin by taking photographs of each student. Encourage each to be the "director" to tell how and where the children should be standing or working. Other photos might show students engaged in cooperative groups or playing chess at recess. These pictures—along with written descriptions—increase during the year to include pictures or drawings of class trips, guests who visit the classroom, and other events that celebrate the students' year.

   Send the book home from time to time and include blank pages at the back for parents to write their comments.

4. ***Conduct Student-to-Student Interviews.*** Teach children how to interview each other. This is a wonderful way for them to get acquainted. Help them formulate questions that go beyond the "favorite color, food, or sports." Model active listening and accurate reporting.

   Students could ask one another who their heroes or heroines are, what famous person they would like to invite for Thanksgiving dinner, how they would solve a pollution problem, or where they would like most to live when they get older. The information they learn could be written on leaves that make up a tree in bloom or on squares that fit together for a quilt.

5. **Read Aloud Appropriate Books.** Read aloud books that focus on issues that might concern students during the first weeks of school. These issues might include making new friends or knowing the expectations in a new class. Reading aloud also provides the opportunity for dialogue. What surprised you about this story? Would you have solved this problem differently? What do you think would happen if the story went on? What are some questions that begin a dialogue when there is no "right" answer? Examples of good books to read during the first weeks of school include:

K-3   **Will I Have A Friend?** Miriam Cohen
       The Art Lesson, Tomie DePaola
       Friends, Helme Heine
       Alfie Gives A Hand, Shirley Hughes

4-6   **Nothing's Fair in Fifth Grade**, Barthe De Clements
       In the Year of the Boar and Jackie Robinson, Bette Bao Lord
       Amazing Grace, Grace Hoffman

The Third Week:
Teach Democracy Through Class Meetings

Rita Daniels teaches second grade in a small suburban school in the southwest. During the third week of school she calls the students together for their first class meeting. She asks them to carry their chairs to an area in the back of the room and to arrange their chairs in a circle, because in a circle everyone can see everyone else. The message here is that every voice counts.

"How do we want our classroom to be this year?" she begins.

Everyone wants a turn. Every child has an idea. Rita encourages the students to phrase their suggestions as positive statements.

"Take turns," someone offers.

"Use nice language when you talk to other kids," another says.

"If you volunteer to do a job, make sure you finish it."

"Say *thank you* if someone gives you something."

Rita is careful to write the statement exactly as the student says it. "If I want the student to rephrase her suggestion or to clarify her thinking I ask her to say more. I don't change a word of what she says, because I want her to know that I respect her suggestion just the way she framed it."

WHAT A CLASS MEETING CAN DO

❋ *Allows children to consider choices or viewpoints other than their own.*

❋ *Provides an opportunity to state problems in a way that others can understand.*

❋ *Gives students a forum to reflect on the experience of the meeting.*

What Do Class Meetings Promote?

Caring Language and Behavior

When Rita asks her class "How do we want our classroom to be this year?"; she uses *we* because it is inclusive. It tells her students that the ownership for their behavior will be shared.

Sometimes students will use "gripe" language to describe situations or problems. "Peter never listens to anyone," or "Sara Beth doesn't finish her work and we all get in trouble."

When she hears this, Rita models more inclusive problem posing. "Are you asking," Rita will say, "'How can I encourage people to be better listeners?'" She not only demonstrates ways to turn "gripes" into questions but also reminds students to use "I" in their questions.

Thoughtful Dialogue

Students need to engage in discussions that involve real-life problem solving. For example, Mariette Hartley's fourth graders discussed the number of guests to invite to their author's tea in early October. Their initial decision was to have parents, grandparents, and the rest of the school, but they had to narrow their original list after visiting the school library and estimating the number of guests who could comfortably sit in the room. Mariette could have made the decision for them more quickly, but she would have denied them the opportunity to come to their own conclusions. Students become responsible decision makers *only* when *they* make decisions.

Problem-Solving Prosocial Skills

Rita Daniels is convinced that class meetings are most valuable when they are held on a regular basis. The framework of a democratic meeting provides ongoing opportunities to practice the values of democracy. Rita is realistic about the limitations on her time and tries to set aside a half hour each week for the meeting. Some weeks, however, she finds that she needs to have a short meeting daily, particularly if she uses the meetings as forums for problem solving. For example, she may have a meeting on how to deal with bullies in the playground.

> **WHEN YOU REFLECT ON THE MEETING WITH YOUR STUDENTS, REMEMBER TO:**
> * *give positive feedback*
> * *make eye contact with the whole group*
> * *try to think of ideas or suggestions that haven't yet been shared*

Acknowledge and Validate Caring Behavior

The agenda of the class meeting is the curriculum, but prosocial behavior is the vehicle through which the content is learned. Skills of behavior need to be taught, acknowledged, and validated so that students can construct the knowledge that prosocial behavior is the fuel that permits a class meeting to run efficiently.

Rita validates this behavior when she ends class meetings with a round-robin reflection. She might ask, "How did someone show respect to you or to someone else today?" "How were you a responsible member of our classroom community today?" "Did someone show kindness or concern for you this week? Did you show these to anyone?"

Additional Real-Life Questions for Class Meetings

1. How shall we behave when a substitute teacher is in the room? It is best to establish positive expectations before you anticipate a change in routine. Discussions like this—before the fact—give students the signal that responsible behavior is essential.

2. What are some of the problems you've been having in the lunchroom (during this morning's assembly, on the bus)? Students need to know that consistent behavior is valued in every corner of the school.

3. Which one of our class rules do we need to talk about more? This is a wonderful opportunity to discuss what we mean by respect, for example. Through demonstration and positive reinforcement we can help students recognize the importance of showing respect toward one's self, one's partner, and the school community.

4. Should we try to reduce the amount of paper we waste in class? How can we do this? Environmental issues take on another meaning when students are able to measure the difference their problem solving makes.

5. What should I—the teacher—do about students who interrupt me while I'm working with other students? We can use class meetings to let students know that we have problems too and that they can help.

6. What issues or concerns do you have? Encourage students to add to the class meeting agenda. For example, Tamar had a problem with being excluded from small-group games on the playground. She wanted the class to talk about this: "This is not just my problem. I've noticed that other kids get left out from lots of things too."

Suppose Things Don't Work Easily. What If . . .

A Student Doesn't Listen When I'm Speaking?

Stop talking. Wait for the student to look at you. Resume talking right where you left off. Do not repeat what you said, because the student will soon learn that she doesn't have to attend the first time, that you will always repeat what she has missed. However, consider rephrasing what you were saying later in the conversation. In this way students who were listening will have a chance to hear the information presented in another way, and the child who did not pay attention will have a chance to hear the information so that he has the opportunity to catch up.

Make sure that you have an opportunity to compliment the child for something else soon. This gives the whole class the message that you are not angry at her.

In a caring classroom the teacher does not give confusing messages by calling on children to answer a question when the teacher knows the student wasn't listening. Nonverbal clues and consistent adult behavior serve as better reminders to all students.

A Child Doesn't Present His Thoughts Clearly?

"Kevon, hold that thought." Kevon has presented an idea during a class meeting that few children can understand. Try to let him present his entire anecdote or thought (although sometimes it's not possible!).

Turn to other students. "How would you say the same idea, Cory?"

"How would you say it, Bill?"

"How would you say it, Juan?"

"Kevon, which one do you like best? Try it out for yourself." Kevon gets the idea that there are more concise ways to present his views and that he will have a chance to choose a more effective way. The rest of the class learns to support Kevon's effort by offering him a menu to choose from.

A Child Talks Too Long?

Wait until later in the day and ask the students for suggestions. "Let's suppose someone in the group talks too long. How can you tell a person in a respectful way that they're going on too long?'

Rachel: "John, could we hear from Maria now? She hasn't had a chance yet."

Quincy: "Would it be okay if we give someone else a turn?"

Dallas: " Could we go on to the next thing?"

Students practice the various responses with partners. They know that it is disrespectful to interrupt someone in the middle of a sentence. They learn the importance of a pleasant, nonthreatening tone of voice when making requests of others. Make sure that ample time is allotted for practicing these delicate skills.

There Are Too Many Suggestions and Not Enough Time?

"I'll take three questions and three comments." This limits the number of children who speak in the group. If there are students who still wish to speak, teach them to say, "If you have anything else to say to me, please see me later." This is effective whether it is the teacher or a classmate who is speaking.

Students Don't Understand but Won't Ask for Help?

Focus on the language you expect to hear and validate it when you hear it.

Claudia is obviously confused. "I don't get it," she tells you.

You say: "I love the way you said that. Would you repeat it?" or:

"Thanks for asking. You're letting me know how to help you when you tell me that you don't get it."

Once students know how to express their insecurities a huge burden seems to be lifted. Acknowledge their willingness to tell you that they don't know. Demonstrate or role-play ways to say "I don't understand." Thank students when they tell you that they "don't get it" just as you would thank them for remembering to use any academic skill you have taught them.

Include Parents from the Start

Successful schools recognize that parents and teachers working together create the best learning conditions for the child. Too often parents receive watered down versions or incomplete accounts of what's happening in their classroom. Almost every parent knows the scene: Your child came home from school. After you greet him and offer a snack you ask, "How was school today?"

"Okay."

"What did you do?"

"Nothing."

Imagine how a teacher who has worked hard to create a meaningful and coherent

---

The First Newsletter

Dear Parents,

This year we plan to create a classroom community that will help all of the students become responsible and caring members of our democratic society. We will focus on ways to include respect and responsibility, kindness, concern, and trust in all that we do.

The students and I will contribute to a monthly newsletter called the *Fourth Grade All Stars*. In it we will tell you what we are studying, what activities we have included to reinforce our studies, and ways that you can get involved with your child's progress. Sometimes your child might ask you to be part of homework assignments by discussing with him or her your opinion about some things we have discussed in class, or your own school memories. Sometimes we'll ask you to listen to your child read a story and talk with him about what he has read. These assignments should not take more that thirty minutes to complete.

We believe that when a child knows that home and school are working together toward the same goals we will, indeed, have created a caring classroom community.

Sincerely,

---

school day would respond to such information!

One of the best ways to avoid such misinformation is to begin the year by letting parents know that your intent is to create a caring classroom community and that their support and encouragement is part of creating such a community. Assure them that you will keep them informed by sending home newsletters (or whatever form of communication you think is most valuable on a regular basis).

Typical Homework Assignments for Parents and Children

1. ***Discuss the Guidelines.*** After you have completed your guidelines for behavior, have the students write them down (or copy them for younger students). Send the sheet home and ask students to interview their parents by having the parents answer some of the following questions:

   ❈ What do you think of our guidelines?

   ❈ Do you think that this is the way adults behave at work?

   ❈ How have you seen me use these behaviors at home?

   ❈ Can we draw a picture together that shows us practicing one of these guidelines at home?

2. ***Read a Story Together.*** Ask students to take home a favorite story to read to parents. Ask parents to tell the child the funniest (scariest, most memorable, earliest memory) story from the grown-up's childhood. Ask the child to illustrate a scene from his parents' story.

3. ***Talk about School's Practical Value.*** Ask students to interview parents regarding how they use mathematics in their daily lives. Alternatively, ask them how they use information about history, geography, or science in their lives. Have students draw a picture of their parent using math.

4. ***Enjoy Poetry.*** Send home a poem in two voices. Parent and child can read it together. If language or reading pose a problem, send home a poem in one voice to be read to parents (or translate the poem into the parents' native language). Ask the parent and child to write a poem in two voices together. (A wonderful resource is Paul Fleischman's *Joyful Noise: Poems for Two Voices*, HarperCollins, 1988).

From the first moment of the first morning of the first day of school students begin to construct a model of what it means to be a member of a caring classroom. Teacher-made posters, calm and well-modulated voices, a recognition that all opinions matter—all help children construct the knowledge that they are valued members of this classroom. Teachers and parents who agree that the values of a caring community are the cornerstones of a democracy provide a consistency and coherence that continue to guide all of our children.

Action Plan: How Can I Encourage Caring Today?

Make an audio tape of one class meeting with your students. As you listen to it reflect on the following:

* Your tone of voice.

* The words you use to convey care.

* The amount of time you wait before student's answer. Research shows that the longer the wait time, the more students respond and the more elaborate their answers.

What goal will you set for yourself the next time you have a class meeting?

CHAPTER THREE

Toward a Caring Curriculum

Your own learning experiences are a good way to think about how to incorporate care into the curriculum. If one was to describe learning to do something well, the description might include learning to drive a car, diaper a baby, or play the piano. Each of these experiences would probably contain the following characteristics:

❉ You knew why you were learning:

"All of my friends were driving when they were sixteen."

"The baby would be wet if I didn't learn how fit the diaper to her body."

"My parents made me play the piano at first, and it was a good way to get out of washing the dishes!"

※ You knew what "good work" looked like, because you could see examples or models of others who performed the task well.

※ You could engage in *dialogue* that allowed you to think about what you were doing and what goals you wanted to achieve.

※ You had opportunities to *practice*, to self-assess and to self-correct, so that you could eventually perform the task by yourself.

※ You may have been praised for your efforts and budding expertise, which bolstered your confidence.

※ The work in which you engaged was *real* in the sense that it was meaningful to you.

HOW TO STRENGTHEN CURRICULUM DEVELOPMENT

1. *Help Students Recognize That Learning is a Human Construction. Our experiences and beliefs shape the meaning we make out of every new experience. Learning is contextual, emergent, messy, and nonlinear.*

2. *Engage in Honest Dialogue to Check Frequently for Understanding. Students are the authority of their own knowledge. Find out what they know and assume it to be true.*

3. *Take Students' Ideas Seriously. When you receive the idea you receive the student as well.*

4. *Build in Ample Opportunities for Students to Share What They Have Learned. Much of our learning is in the explaining. Teachers are often the ones who learn the material the best—let students teach.*

It is not so difficult to believe that students will work hard when they care about the work. If children see value in what they are doing teachers are less likely to rely on external rewards and punishments. The following examples show how others have made the principles of caring the foundation of their existing curricula.

Caring Across the Curriculum

Reading

Reading Aloud: Modeling How To Care About Social Values

Reading a story aloud is not intended to compete with your school's established reading program. Rather, we read stories to children to focus on the characteristics of caring (in addition to other goals). We want students to hear and discuss how values such as kindness, concern, honesty, respect, and responsibility are part of the human condition. We want children to make connections to what they know and understand. What's more, the stories we read aloud give the whole class a common experience for discussions that follow. (See chapter four for additional strategies that encourage dialogue.)

Become a Storyteller Yourself

On a sunny morning in November I sat on top of my desk and faced my fourth graders. I was about to tell them how I felt after reading *NightJohn* by Gary Paulsen. I hoped that I would not cry when I described the emotions that this story evoked. I mentally ticked off what I wanted to say and realized that a lump had begun to form in my throat. I realized that I seldom let my students see the passion that good books elicited in me. I told them about my feelings often enough, but they hardly ever saw me moved by a good story. I proceeded, confident that my emotions would be as great a motivator as my words. My story began:

"Many years ago I worked with teachers in a country in southeast Asia where it was very safe to live. People could walk with confidence through any neighborhood at any time of the day or night. There was no crime, because anyone who committed a crime was hanged. No one owned guns. There was virtually no unemployment, and everyone was guaranteed a home. The whole country was clean and neat and safe.

"Doesn't that sound just about perfect? There was just one catch, however. There was no freedom of speech. Citizens and reporters were not allowed to speak against the government. University professors were expelled from the country if they said anything against the ruling party. Men and women who were in prison for speaking out were granted a trial by judges who already knew their fate.

"From that time on I have wondered how to teach about democracy and the freedoms that our constitution guarantees. If we have never been anything but free how can we know the difference? Last night, when I finished reading NightJohn by Gary Paulsen, I thought I found my answer.

"NightJohn is a slave who escaped north to freedom but who came back to the South on his own. He came back to teach reading to other slaves. NightJohn knew that the penalty for teaching reading was dismemberment—removing limbs from the body. But he returned anyway."

I opened the book to the inside cover and read the note from author Gary Paulsen:

"The research for this short book took over five years and it was heartbreaking. At many times, reading through the slave narratives, I would find myself crying quietly, weeping for them, for the very real people I have tried to portray in this story. They wanted only one thing—to be free—and they knew reading, learning to read, was the best way to freedom.

It still is..."

My eyes were moist as I recalled the power of this story. I could feel every student's eye riveted to my face. "What would *you* do to preserve the freedoms that America guarantees us?" I asked quietly.

I read *NightJohn* aloud to my students, not only as a way of encouraging them to value reading, but also to encourage them to take seriously their responsibility to help one another.

WHY READING ALOUD IS ESSENTIAL IN A CARING CLASSROOM

❊ *It allows teachers to share stories that demonstrate caring.*

❊ *It provides a common language and experience for class discussions that focus on attributes of care.*

❊ *It allows us to help students of all abilities make their own connections with the story; each student is validated for who he is inside and outside the classroom.*

❊ *It suggests home activities that invite parents to continue the dialogue about caring behavior.*

❊ *It presents teachers with opportunities to model skills that are present when one cares for literature.*

Other Reading Activities that Promote Social Understanding

Create Units by Starting with One Good Book

Instead of teaching a unit on "our community" as she had in the past (trips to the bakery, the post office, the fire department, for example), one second grade teacher read *The Hundred Dresses* by Eleanor Estes to begin a discussion about the homeless. She then asked, "What do you already know about the homeless?" "Where have you gotten your information?" "What other ways could we get more information?"

Students brought in newspaper and magazine pictures of homeless people. They worked in groups to generate lists of characteristics of the homeless they inferred from the photographs. Then they interviewed family members, their principal, a member of their state assembly, and other students to find out what they thought about homeless people. As they added to their original list the second graders were confused to see that there was such a wide range of opinions and beliefs. They also came to understand that the word *homeless* represents a more complex idea than they first thought.

The children decided to build a scale model of their town. They used empty boxes and cans to re-create the fire house, police station, banks, bakery, and parks. One group suggested that they include a place for the homeless people to live, and the class set about to figure out where it should go and how it would look. During this time the teacher read aloud stories that focused on kids who made a difference in their communities by getting involved. The stories gave students a genuine opportunity to explore questions that had real meaning for them.

QUESTIONS TO ASK CHILDREN THAT PROMOTE ANALYSIS AND EVALUATION

"Can young kids like you really make a difference in the world?"

"What suggestions do you have for members of our community, such as the police, firefighters, restaurant owners, churches, and synagogues regarding the homeless?"

"What did you learn about yourself as a learner now that we have completed our unit?"

The second graders told us that they learned that many problems do not have one right or wrong answer and that it is not always easy to separate fact from opinion. The teacher found that students demonstrated empathy and care for others in ways that a social studies textbook could never elicit.

Delve Into History

Third graders worked in cooperative groups to discover how values such as kindness and concern for others have been taught in schools during the past hundred years. The teacher collected reprints of *McGuffey's Readers*, *Fun With Dick and Jane* basal readers, and several other old third grade reading textbooks that she found in the local library and at flea markets. Once each week during this time their teacher read aloud several stories that were popular with today's children. Together, they discussed questions such as: "Do you think stories can teach children to be kinder? To care more about others?" "Has a story made you or someone you know kinder?" "If you were going to examine a story like a scientist, to see if it taught about kindness, what would you look for ?"

Each group in this third grade class decided that they would choose one story from each resource and look closely at the vocabulary. They would also try to figure out whether the moral really contributed to teaching kindness. The third graders thought of themselves as detectives. They were out to solve a mystery: What did the authors want us to learn and did they succeed?

Later, when the teacher read aloud, she chose modern tales that also focused on kindness. They compared and contrasted the old and new stories. She encouraged students to ask parents to share a time when they were treated kindly. Then children were to discuss the differences and similarities between the modern tale and the anecdotes from parents. Not only did the teacher report that her class read more critically as a result of this assignment, but she also saw that highlighting the ingredients of kindness and concern made for the most cohesive class she ever had.

Discuss Responsible Actions

A fifth grade class was plagued by lunchtime brawls. Every day, it seemed, two or more students were punished for hitting or punching other students or for using bad language. Their teacher decided to try using literature to focus on the value of responsibility. Her goal was to help students acknowledge and accept responsibility for their actions.

* ❋ *Read Aloud.* The teacher read aloud *Cracker Jackson*, a story by Betsy Byars, in which Cracker has to make some difficult decisions when he learns that his former baby-sitter is being abused by her husband.

* ❋ *Role Play.* Students role-played central scenes in the story. They frequently reversed roles and played the scene a second time. The discussion focused on what it was like to "be in another person's shoes."

* ❋ *Work in Various Groups.* Students worked in pairs, then in groups of four, and finally in groups of eight to tell their own stories: 'When did you have to make a really difficult decision and what did you do?"

* ❋ *Conduct Interviews.* Students were asked to interview someone from home: "Did you ever have to make a hard decision and weren't sure what to do? How did you finally make a decision? If you had to do it again would you make the same decision?"

* ❋ *Collect and Share Data.* Only then did the teacher begin to help his students make connections between what they discovered about responsible decision making and the choices they were making on the playground.

* ❋ *Deal with Special Problems.* One student quietly asked for help in controlling his impulsivity. The class voted to institute a conflict resolution program in their school. At the teacher's suggestion, they presented a well-developed proposal to the principal and invited parents. Later, several of the biggest troublemakers even volunteered to serve as peer mediators.

Other Ways to Infuse the Curriculum with Curiousity and Concern

Math

Show You Care About Ideas: Chris Reilley introduced a math lesson on finding the area of an object by giving every student in his sixth grade class a maple leaf and an oak leaf that were about the same size. The leaves came from the trees around the school and many were in the reds, yellows, and bright oranges of the autumn.

"I've given you these leaves, because I wanted all of you to continue your work on calculating areas. We've spent some time during the week figuring out the area of everything in our classroom, from the tops of your desks to the room itself. But these leaves intrigued me, because they don't have neat and even sides. Few things in the natural world do. I thought it might be a challenge to look at the area of something that wasn't regular."

Tip: *Students need to know us teachers as problem posers. They need to hear that we care about ideas and that caring leads us to be persistent in working until we are satisfied the job is well done.*

"What I'd like to know is this: Which leaf has the biggest area and how do you know?" Chris had graph paper, Unifix cubes, rulers, and transparent paper available for the students to use. "You can work by yourself or with a partner if you'd like." While the students worked Chris circled the room. He served as a tutor to those students who didn't know how to begin, a coach to those who needed to get to the next step, and a cheerleader to those students who were able to work on the challenge without him.

Tip: *Students need to know that we care about them as much as we care about the curriculum. There is a meaning to what we do, a purpose for our actions. We consider who each student is and what would best serve his or her needs and interests.*

The next day, after the class had completed the task and talked about various ways to find an answer to the leaf problem, Chris asked them to make up their own problems about finding areas in the natural world. He did not ask them to solve the problems; he was first interested in seeing whether they understood the underlying principles.

"Work in your task groups and come to a consensus on the problem you want to submit," he directed.

On the third day, Chris chose to solve the most complicated problem that was submitted. He copied the problem for everyone, and then he proceeded to think aloud. "Boy, this is a tough one. I think I could find the area of this daisy, but first I have to find the area of each petal. And then I've got to figure out the area of the center."

Chris proposed a way to determine the area of the first petal. "Wait a minute!" he said after sharing the solution. "Let's see how many petals are the same size as this one I just worked on. . . ."

Chris Reilley chose to think aloud about math,

To encourage problem-solving, Jean Nicastro invited her kindergartners to chart the kinds of shoes they were wearing.

because he often overheard students ask, "Who cares about this stuff?" As the year progressed and he continued to model caring behavior toward the work, the students' attitude about becoming problem solvers and problem posers improved.

Other Ways to Demonstrate Problem Posing

1. When the students have returned to their seats after lunch, drop a pile of junk mail from home on your desk. "I'm tired of this. What can I do to stop this junk mail from filling up my mailbox every day?"

2. Take your class outside in the winter. "I've noticed that the birds are all out of the seeds from our bird feeders. What could we do out here to feed the birds but not the squirrels?"

3. Early in November tell your students: "My whole family is coming for Thanksgiving dinner and I've got a real problem. How can I teach until the day before the holiday and still entertain my children, my sister, and my mother and my father?"

Social Studies

Social Studies: Caring Citizens Of a Democracy

What is it that makes us Americans? In a diverse society it is often easier to describe how we are different than the ways we are alike. We Americans do not share a common race, religion, or language. We do not share common political views. What binds Americans together is a belief in our guaranteed freedoms. We share a history that values our right to worship, speak, and vote as we choose. We believe in an ideal that says all people are created equal, and we strive for full respect for each of our citizens.

These democratic values—respect for the rights of the individual, opportunities to make informed decisions, responsibility to maintain the common good—are the same ones that we focus on in the caring classroom. It was at this intersection of the two ideals that led Rick Samuels to create a "Celebration of Our Lives."

A Case Study: Fourth Graders and the Doing of Democracy

Rick's fourth-grade students studied famous Americans every year. Rick was always pleased with the activities and projects his students completed, and satisfied that he was exploring famous Americans from diverse backgrounds. But he worried their study didn't go deep enough into an exploration of the prejudice some of these famous individuals had to overcome.

Rick decided to shift the focus of the unit. First, he moved from a statement-based curriculum ("We're going to study famous Americans and their contributions to our democracy") to an inquiry-based curriculum ("In a democracy, who 'owns' knowledge?"). He wanted his students to consider many points of view, to make connections with their own lives, and to care about the impact they could have on the community.

> When we ask questions of the curriculum students do what historians do: gather data, analyze the information, pose questions and offer conclusions based on the best available information. They are no longer consumer of knowledge. They are now the producers.

Next, he displayed photos of people—people of color, the elderly, waitresses, farmers, people in urban settings, construction workers, men and women wearing business suits, homeless people, blonds, brunettes, and so on—and invited his students to give their off-the-cuff impressions of each of them. Who is rich? Who is poor? Who is educated? Who is not? Who is smart? Who is happy? Who is honest? What assumptions are you making based on this single image? This led to a discussion of stereotypes, and how stereotypes are often perpetuated by those in power—the "owners" of knowledge, whether they exist in the media, on Madison Avenue, or on Capitol Hill. Rick brought this discussion to bear on the lives of the famous Americans they were studying. What stereotypes might each one have confronted? He helped make students aware that there are always at least two sides of every story—whether in history or on the nightly news.

A Question-Driven Curriculum

Rick created this curriculum to serve as a vehicle through which students could practice informed, participatory decision-making while learning about the pursuit of truth and freedom of expression. He organized the desks into learning stations so that students could work in small groups. Each station contained up-to-date periodicals that represented a variety of viewpoints, as well as audio-cassettes and trade books on African American history, immigrants, the civil rights movement, women's history, and so on. Each day or two the groups moved to a different stations to survey the material and began to pose questions that they wished to pursue in depth. He encouraged students to keep asking themselves: Who gets to tell the story? Are there other versions of the story? How could these versions be told?

Suggest Exciting Projects

Rick asked his students if they would like to tell their stories through photographs. His students were labeled "at risk." They did not like to write and did not feel successful in writing. They were, however, enthusiastic about the idea of using cameras to show what they knew. That was one reason he proposed that the class create an exhibition dedicated to sharing their photographs of people they feel contribute to society.

Set Students to Work

Rick gave each student a 35-mm camera and a roll of black-and-white film. When they completed shooting the film he had each developed into a contact sheet. After students made their final choice, Rick offered to enlarge each one and to help display the photographs. He suggested that in order to answer the initial question of the unit, each student needed to write the story of the photograph. The class agreed. They wanted their audience to care as much about the work as they did. They understood that they had a responsibility to tell the whole story.

> Use the language of the writing process to teach that different forms of communication can use the same framework:
>
> 1. *Students can* brainstorm *ideas on how to photograph their families and friends.*
> 2. *Students can consider each photograph they take a rough draft.*
> 3. *Students* can edit *their contact sheets* in peer groups.
> 4. *Students can chose their final photograph using a set of* criteria *that the class formulates together.*

Teach Mini-Lessons

Rick listened carefully as the students' attempted to answer "who 'owns' knowledge?" He spent time during each social studies class teaching mini-lessons based on the skills that groups of students needed to complete their tasks (Sample mini-lessons: How to tell a story using only one picture; How to decide what to leave out in a photo or an essay). He used class meetings to further the dialogue about how powerful a pen, a camera, and a story can be.

Hold Reception for Parents

In April, several months after the unit began, parents and friends were invited to the opening reception at city hall for the "Celebration of Our Lives." The fifth-grade string quartet was invited to serenade visitors. Punch and cookies were served. Parents who, in the past, came to school to receive unpleasant news about their children's work, swelled with pride as they saw the care and attention that was lavished upon the participants in the project. This unit was rigorous and intellectually-driven.

Adapting the Unit for Young Children

You can adapt this unit to the age and needs of your students.

❋ *Draw Pictures.* Very young children might draw pictures of the family or friends they wish to celebrate. Have them divide the paper into quarters or eighths and make a small sketch in each block. After the page is "edited" ask them to enlarge their choice on large paper.

❀ *Make Collages.* Younger students might make collages from magazine pictures and postcards. The focus would be on telling the story of their families or friends who would then be invited to school to share in the story retelling.

❀ **Take a Tour of Your Neighborhood.** Visit the police, the fire fighters, the owners of stores along the way. Ask groups of students to draw each of the people they meet. Ask others to interview them. Create a museum of these people called "Celebrating Our Town." Make sure you invite the subjects to visit the musuem.

Strategies Embedded In The Curriculum "Who 'Owns' Knowledge?"

1. *Clarified Purpose.* Rick made explicit the purpose for and the value of the task. He showed students where it fit into the big picture of learning skills, behaviors, and ideas that are esteemed in the real world. He provided visual maps and diagrams for students to "see" how their ideas are valued and how they connected to other principles of the caring community.

2. *Defined Quality Work.* Rick spent time talking with his students about what quality work looks like. Together they decided which criteria to include to remind them of the indicators of "good" work. Rick proved that students who participate in creating rubrics feel a greater sense of ownership in a project.

3. *Emphasized Self Assessment.* He provided students with the opportunity to practice ongoing self-assessment and self-correction. Rick trusted that each student—with his modeling and coaching to support their efforts—knew what good work looked like and what they needed to do to work toward that goal.

4. *Built-in Goal Setting.* Rick allowed ample time for reflection and goal setting. Several times during the course of the study he stopped to ask students to write or discuss, "What have I learned about a democracy and about myself as a citizen?" or "What skills have I learned, and how can I use them in other areas of my life?" or "What would I like to do better next time, and how would I proceed?"

Science

Science in the Caring Classroom: Ethical Behavior
A Fifth Grade Class Demonstrates Care for Animals

Each fall I brought my students to the banks of the Hudson River to collect specimens for our classroom aquarium. My third graders loved to see me put on the pair of rubber waders and walk chest-deep into the river. My colleague and I spread a seine net across wide areas of water in the hope of netting a few fish that we could take back to our classroom for further study.

> *Yehosheba:* It's gonna die.
>
> *Me:* How do you know?
>
> *Yehosheba:* I've been watching it every day. And measuring it too. Look at my journal. The numbers are getting smaller every day.
>
> *Me:* What do you propose we do, Yehosheba?
>
> *Yehosheba:* Put it back. Today. Before it dies.
>
> *Me:* Let's ask the class. Will you make a proposal at the class meeting and give your reasons?
>
> *Yehosheba:* Yeah. I'm going to propose that we don't have the right to keep this killifish in the aquarium just so we can watch it die.
>
> *Me:* So, would you like our discussion to focus on our rights and responsibilities as scientists?
>
> *Yehosheba:* Yeah.

That afternoon Yehosheba's concern about the classroom science project was the center of the class meeting. The ethics of caring for living things and our responsibility to those things engaged my third graders for over an hour. The conversation began with Yehosheba's question, "Do we have the right to watch the killifish die just to have specimens to study?" The children—part of a school that valued thoughtful dialogue—were able to ask critical questions of one another and of themselves. Meaning making was a valued part of their curriculum.

Expanded to Hudson River

Yehosheba's concerns about the small killifish encouraged me to add a significant component to the curriculum. In addition to learning about the ecology of the Hudson River, I wanted my students to embark on a journey that would serve as an affirmation of a caring community.

Until Yehosheba voiced her concerns I had never given much thought to the few fish who died in our tank each year. Now I had to recognize that the study of the river was more than exploring the habitat of fish. Yehosheba and her classmates had become involved in a personal, concrete way. They had encouraged me to change forever the way I looked at the curriculum.

Other Activities That Promote an Ethic of Care in the Science Class

1. *Invite scientists* to speak to the class about the difficult decisions they make as part of their work. What guides their decisions? What were the effects of their decisions on their work, their families, their subjects?

2. *Use software* that eliminates the need for laboratory dissection of animals. Discuss the value of using software vs. the value of a hands-on experience. Help children understand when each method might be employed.

3. *Use the Newspaper.* It provides current examples of the ways that science practices values of care, and also reports unethical behavior. Ask students to focus on these articles for a current events assignment.

4. *Evaluate science trade books* from the school library through the lens of caring values. What would students add to each book to emphasize the responsibility of all of us who "do" science?

5. *Return Specimens.* If you study live specimens, return them to their natural habitat when you have completed your work. For example, first graders keep a Hudson River aquarium in their classrooms. Each June they return to the river to release the fish. The children say good-bye while reciting their river odes to the fish.

RIVER ODE TO THE FISH

Good-bye, old hogchoker
Good-bye, dear white perch
You have made us so happy all year
Now, we must be happy too
As we let you go back to the River
And back to your families
Thank you for teaching us so much about yourselves.

—Loretta S.

This is the first letter that Eloise Parente sent home to the parents of her third grade students:

Dear Parents,

A large part of our educational program this year will be to focus on the values of the caring community. These values include kindness and concern, respect, responsibility, honesty, and trustworthiness.

One of the ways I will focus on these values it to read several books aloud to the class. These books will help us have class discussions about the ideas that are raised by the story. Later in the month we will begin to examine the voyages of Christopher Columbus by asking students to pose their own questions that might help us all better understand whether Columbus discovered America, invaded it, or encountered it.

From time to time I will send home activities that you and your child can do together. The purpose for this is to reinforce the class discussions that took place that day and to let the child know that you too value the development of our caring classroom community. No activity should take more than twenty minutes to complete. You will always have several days to complete the activity.

I welcome your suggestions and encourage you to stop by to see what we are doing to create a caring community.

Take the Curriculum Home

It is important to continue sharing with parents ways you will be incorporating values into the curriculum. Parents who understand how you plan to highlight the values of respect, responsibility, concern, honesty, and trustworthiness in the existing curriculum are far more likely to support your goals and to reinforce your efforts.

Activities that Parents and Children Can Do Together

1. *Child Reads to You.* Ask your child to read you *The Wednesday Surprise* by Eve Bunting. In this book, the little girl and her grandmother work hard to give a special birthday present. Tell your child about the best present you ever received from someone. Discuss with your child the many meanings for the word *present*. What else can we give someone that cannot be bought at a store?

2. ***Discuss the Book.*** Read *I Hate My Brother Harry* by Crescent Dragonwagon to your child. Ask your child to tell you about the story and what the little girl did to solve her problem. Choose an issue on which you and your child sometimes disagree. It could be sharing the TV, completing household responsibilities, fighting with siblings, or anything else that causes conflict. Brainstorm possible solutions, discuss the pros and cons of each one, and agree on one solution to try for one week. Draw a "before" and "after" picture together. (Before: I used to. . . After: Now I . . .)

3. ***Listen to your child read*** *Rosie and Michael* by Judith Viorst. Discuss with your child some of the positive characteristics of your own friends. What do you look for in a friend? What are some responsibilities of being a friend? Draw a picture together of you and one of your friends.

4. ***Ask your child to read the following poem.***

THIS IS JUST TO SAY
I have eaten
the plums
that were in
the icebox
and which
you were probably
saving
for breakfast
Forgive me
they were delicious
so sweet
and so cold
—William Carlos Williams

Talk together about anything in the poem that makes you curious. Do you think someone should apologize for something for which they are not really sorry? Did you ever have to do such a thing? How else can members of a caring community behave? Write a poem and illustrate it with something you have just discussed.

5. ***Read Together.*** Read *The Trouble With Mom* by Babette Cole and/or *Daddy Has A Pair of Striped Shorts* by Mimi Otey. These are stories that deal with parents who are different from the norm and how that affects their childrens' attitudes toward them. Discuss whether or not your own parents caused you embarrassment when you were a child and how you resolved the problem. Go back to the story to find evidence that the

children really did care for their parents. How can people in a supportive community learn to accept the differences each member brings? Draw a comic strip or sequence a story by dividing the paper into equal sections to illustrate how two people can resolve their differences.

Action Plan: What Can I Do Today?

Choose a unit in any curricular area to examine closely. Rethink the structure of the unit in one or more of the following ways:

✿ *Pose Problem.* Begin the unit by posing a problem, instead of stating the theme. What is the big idea of the unit? What are additional engaging questions?

✿ *Encourage Independent Thinking.* Provide several opportunities for students to make real decisions about what and how they will demonstrate their understanding of the unit.

✿ *Encourage Self-Evaluation.* Ask students to evaluate all of their work in writing and sign it before turning it in. Use rubrics or other indicators of good work as guides.

✿ *Include a final Reflection Sheet* that encourages kids to think about their learning process by asking, "What did I learn about myself as a learner? What is my goal for the next time I do this?"

CHAPTER FOUR

Promoting Thoughtful Dialogue in the Classroom

We all have assumptions and images in our minds—*mental maps* that others may not share. Students' mental maps may vary, for example, third graders and I had just finished reading the first chapter of *Pixie*, a novel by Matthew Lipman. Pixie tells us that this is not her real name. She says that her real name is the name that her mother and father gave her. "Then what is real?" I asked. The children thought for a few moments, and several hands went up.

I waited until I saw many hands in the air.

"Real is anything that lives and breathes," answered Richard.

"So, is this table real?" I asked.

Richard answered "no"with authority.

Other students disagreed, but Richard didn't budge.

"Isn't this pencil real?"

"No."

"A chair doesn't live, but it's real, isn't it?"

"No."

Richard remained firm. He did not "see" what seemed obvious to the others. Students continued to offer additional support for their point of view, but Richard remained committed to his original statement.

As I listened to the dialogue, I realized that Richard had formed a set of beliefs, a mental map, based on his view of the world. When he participated in the dialogue, Richard learned—maybe for the first time—that his map about "what is real" might be based on assumptions that others did not share.

SUSPENDING ASSUMPTIONS

In the caring classroom we work to suspend our assumptions. Unless we can acknowledge that they exist, and examine them, we will be unable to entertain other points of view. Holding dialogues with children can help.

Mental maps are those deeply held beliefs or pictures in our minds that influence our thinking. Like Richard, we are seldom even aware of them or the effect they have on the way we act and react. The effectiveness of a respectful community is dependent upon how willing each of its members is to confront his or her assumptions. Thoughtful dialogue provides the opportunity to turn the mirror inward.

Using Dialogue to Enhance Learning

How Does Dialogue Differ From Debate?

A debate is a form of discourse in which participants take opposite sides of a specific question. Information in a debate flows in one direction: from the speaker to the listener. The speaker refutes, rebuts, and argues. Either he wins by convincing his opponent that his is the best argument, or he loses.

By contrast, the value of a discussion is that the entire group will come to some kind of understanding by the end. At times, discussions can include debate. The intention is to have everyone on the same side at the end. Good discussions succeed when they move beyond the point where the group began. There is an agreement that forward motion has occurred.

Dialogue is the fuel that drives the values-oriented classroom. It is focused on exploring ideas. Compared with debate and discussion, there is no intention at closure. We never really get "there," because as we pool our group understanding it constantly changes and grows. There are no winners or losers in a dialogue.

How Is Dialogue Different From Traditional Class Discussions?

When we engage in meaningful dialogue:

✤ The focus of the conversation is on the ideas of a text rather than on its facts.

✤ There is no agenda, no lesson to be taught.

✤ The teacher trades her mastery of the content for mastery of the process.

✤ There is no commitment to "right" answers; the commitment is to support reasoned opinions and ideas with textual evidence.

✤ There is a deliberate attempt to value all voices by attending to classroom environment.

Dialogue is embedded in inquiry and reflection. Each participant examines her own assumptions as well as the collective thinking of the group. A dialogue has power when members of the group come to know that they are smarter as a collective than they are when they think alone.

A class of fifth grade special education students read an excerpt from Machiavelli's *The Prince*. Their teacher told me that the kids would never be able to discuss such a difficult text. I convinced her to let me try.

After I read the page with the students I asked my opening question, "Would this man make a good principal for your school?" The students didn't hesitate. Their conversation compared Machiavelli's ideas with the qualities they valued in a principal. They read and reread many of the same sentences for the purpose of supporting their ideas, and they did so without complaining about reading or listening to a repetition of the lines. In all, this was a wonderful dialogue—spirited and passionate.

At the end, as I was about to leave, I saw one boy punch another lightly on his forearm. "Hey! We're not so dumb after all, are we?"

DIALOGUE IS A VALUABLE STRATEGY IN THE COMPASSIONATE CLASSROOM BECAUSE:

✤ *Dialogue promotes an open-minded consideration of everyone's ideas.*

✤ *Dialogue encourages students to know and understand ideas by constructing them rather than receiving them from another source.*

✤ *Dialogue makes our internal conversations explicit. Thinking, speaking, and writing are separate processes. Often we don't know what our thinking sounds like until we say it out loud.*

✤ *Dialogue values differences. In a classroom community we value each other's differences rather than fear them.*

Getting Started with Dialogue

First Things First

1. ***Choose a Text.*** A text provides us with a common vocabulary and a common experience. Texts should be chosen because they provide rich and/or ambiguous words or ideas. A common text allows us to consider

our own experiences but only as a means of making meaning. Texts help to keep the dialogue from dissolving into personal opinions.

Places to find texts include:

- ❋ trade books
- ❋ bumper stickers
- ❋ political cartoons
- ❋ T-shirts
- ❋ videos
- ❋ graffiti
- ❋ music (printed words or on tape)
- ❋ art prints
- ❋ dance performances
- ❋ comic strips

Choose engaging, values-oriented texts.

2. ***Arrange the Seats in a Circle.*** A circle is the only configuration that allows all to see everyone else. I have found that chairs are better than the floor. Seats keep all students in place so that each of them can be seen throughout the dialogues.

3. ***Ask an Opening Question*** that encourages students to connect with the text.

   Generic opening questions that foster dialogue:

   - ❋ "Does the moral of the story relate in any way to our classroom?" (This encourages the students to make connections and to see differences as well as similarities.)

   - ❋ "How does this (story, poem, art print, etc.) compare or contrast with the one we read last week?" (This question connects the ideas raised during prior discussions.)

   - ❋ "From the list of words I have written on the chart, choose one characteristic of care that the main character exhibits." (Asking for choices promotes analysis and evaluation.)

4. ***Ask follow-up questions*** that build on students' prior responses. With practice you will begin to sense when to listen to students engage with one another and when to move the dialogue forward.

   Some questions that you might use to move the dialogue forward:

   - ❋ What reasons do you have for saying that?

✿ Are you agreeing or disagreeing with the student who spoke?

✿ Could you assume the opposite is also true?

✿ Do you think it would happen that way again? Why or why not?

5. *Ask Clarifying Questions.* Instead of assuming you know what a student means ask:

✿ Do you mean. . .?

✿ Are you saying. . .?

✿ How does your idea connect with. . . (another passage in the text or to another idea)?

✿ How are you defining that word?

6. *Leave Time for Reflection Afterward.* Ask students to reflect aloud. Group reflection makes the internal dialogue explicit. It helps kids to know that they do know. Sometimes students who don't choose to participate in a dialogue will be willing to reflect on the process. Try these reflective questions: "What did you notice or observe about our conversation today? How was it like or different from the others we've had?"

WHAT OTHER QUESTIONS CAN STUDENTS ASK THEMSELVES?

✿ *How well did I listen attentively to others' ideas?*

✿ *Did I allow time for thought after asking a question or making a response?*

✿ *Did I wait until others finished their complete thought before I entered the dialogue?*

✿ *Did I ask for clarification if I did not understand another's ideas?*

✿ *Was I able to build on another person's ideas rather than adding new ones?*

✿ *What did I learn about myself in this dialogue?*

A Beginning Dialogue With Fourth Graders

The following dialogue was generated after my fourth graders finished reading *The Girl Who Loved the Wind* by Jane Yolen (Harper Trophy, 1972).

". . .And the last thing he saw was the billowing cape as Danina and the wind sailed far to the west into the ever-changing world."

The fourth graders' delight with the story was apparent. They applauded when I closed the book.

"I'm glad you liked the story. I invite you to participate in a conversation with me. The question is: Do you think that Danina had a right to leave her father so that she could follow the wind?"

I try to use phrases like "invite you to participate" to set a tone that implies comfort and trust. If no one answers right away, I wait. Sometimes students need time to think, sometimes they need to make sure the situation is a safe one for risk-taking. Since there is no "right" answer I seldom call on a child if she does not volunteer. When I do, I ask permission.

"I see four hands. Five. Seven. Eight. . ."

I seldom call on the first person who volunteers. Even when several hands are in the air I continue to wait. When I do I am always gratified to see many more hands. Although I can only call on one child at a time, I try to remember who volunteered so that I can ask some of them to agree or disagree with the opening answer.

"I think that Danina did have the right to leave her father." Paula answers quickly and then remains silent.

"Because. . .," I begin.

I try to use the word "because" to help students extend their thinking. The word offers a stem to build on, and doesn't feel as demanding to some as asking, "why?"

The dialogue continues with Desmond. "I think she shouldn't have left her father, because he loved her so much that he made sure that nothing bad would ever happen to her."

"Do you disagree with Paula?" I ask. "Tell her. Say, 'I disagree with you, Paula.'"

I model how students should look at the person they wish to address and how they might begin speaking. "I disagree with you Paula," encourages the speaker to look at Paula and not at me. My goal is to demonstrate how to disagree without being disagreeable.

I notice that Samori has been waving his hand in the air since I first asked the question. I recognize him by nodding my head in his direction and saying:

"Thanks for waiting, Samori."

"That's okay," he tells me.

When I know that someone has waited a while, I make sure to thank him or her for waiting. This acknowledgment gives the message to Samori and to the rest of the class that I have noticed him and that I value patient waiting.

"Well, what I think is that the wind was right. I mean. . .every day should be different." Samori's voice trails off. "I don't know. . ." he adds.

"I disagree with everybody," Kyle begins

I immediately intervene. "Hold on, Kyle. Let Samori finish." I turn to Samori. "Yes, you do know."

I look at the whole class.

"Thanks for giving Samori the time to think. These are hard questions you're dealing with."

I will not let another child jump in to continue the conversation until the preceding child has completed his entire thought. This lets the class know that I value each child's ideas. In this community it is safe to take the time you need to think your thoughts and then to say them.

The dialogue continues and more students contribute. They agree and disagree with one another. I notice that most speakers remember to make eye contact with the speaker and not with me.

It is time to move the conversation to a higher level; otherwise I'm sure we will end up going back over old territory. I ask: "Now that you have thought about Danina's rights, what about the wind? Did the wind have a responsibility to Danina? After all, she left her home to follow the wind."

My question moves the conversation from the protagonist, Danina, to the antagonist, the wind. My goal is to encourage students to look at all sides of an idea. Ultimately we will talk about the relationship between rights and responsibilities.

"Marilyn, you had a big smile on your face while I was asking that question. Would you like to answer ?"

I pay close attention to body language. Some children feel comfortable simply jumping into a conversation. They should—from time to time—be given that opportunity. Many prefer to raise their hand. But some need to be invited in to the conversation. They give many signs: moving forward in their seats, raising an index finger next to their face, smiling or nodding their head.

Sometimes I misinterpret body language. When this happens I ask if she wants to respond, but the child will usually say no. I apologize and move on.

DIALOGUE WITH YOUNG CHILDREN

At the Westorchard School in Chappaqua, New York, K–3 teachers have been working for many years on dialogues with children. Here are some of their suggestions and experiences:

❋ *A kindergarten teacher asks students to retell the story of* Goldilocks and the Three Bears. *Then she asks, "Would this story be different if Goldilocks were a boy?"*

❋ *Pat Mutalo read her first grade students* The Frozen Land, *which describes the Canadian government's efforts to save the Inuits by transporting them to safety. Then the teacher began her discussion be asking, "Did the government have the right to force the people to leave the land?"*

❋ *A second grade teacher read her class* Fly Away Home, *by Eve Bunting. The question the teacher asked was, "Do you need a house to have a home?"*

❋ *A multiage class listened to* The Big Orange Spot, *by Daniel Pinkwater, the story of a man who is asked by his neighbors to change the color of his house because the neighbors didn't like it. The opening question asked by the teacher was, "Should an individual change if the community thinks he should?"*

Keep in Mind:
The nature of dialogue with young children is quite different than with older students. Young children:

❋ *Can't always sustain a long dialogue.*

❋ *Tend to be more anecdotal.*

❋ *Do much better in small groups.*

Facilitating Honest Dialogue

1. ***Ask Open-ended Questions that You Really Want to Pursue.*** If you only ask questions to which there is one right answer, students will soon learn to play "guess what's on the teacher's mind."

2. ***Leave Your Own Assumptions at the Door.*** Remember that you too enter the dialogue with a set of assumptions. If you are heavily invested in a point of view or if you need to tell students "the truth," then it is better to use a different strategy.

3. ***Learn to Trust the Process.*** Dialogue is slow, messy, and circular. Understanding takes time. Think how many times you have had to go back again and again in order to really understand an idea or concept.

4. ***Build in Time for Reflection at the End of Every Dialogue.*** Reflection strengthens students' metacognitive skills, and helps teachers to learn how well the values of an empathic community have been internalized.

5. ***Recognize that Creating Honest Dialogue Takes Time to Learn.*** As a facilitator, your role is not to have all of the answers. It is not to cover material or to lead students to a conclusion. Your role is to help students construct meaning for themselves.

How Dialogue Serves the Caring Community

Dialogue Helps Us To "See" The Invisible

Each time we present a lesson to students we are, in fact, presenting more than the lesson itself. The "visible" curriculum is one we can all see: the material, projects, and assessments. The "invisible" curriculum can only be felt and experienced: who gets heard, whose voice is valued, who is best served by the form and manner of teaching. Embedded in the invisible curriculum is the culture of your classroom.

Questions to Help You "See" Yourself in Context

❋ Do your own actions model respectful behavior? Do you remember to thank students for the behaviors you see and not for the quality of their answers? Is your tone of voice carefully modulated? Are you fully present when a student speaks to you?

❋ Do you pay attention to the silences between the sounds, the rhythm of the dialogue, the body language of the participants? Observing dialogue as a whole piece as well as each of its parts creates the conditions for a trusting environment.

SCENES THAT CONTRIBUTE TO THE CULTURE OF YOUR CLASSROOM

What to look for:	Possible solution:
1. Who speaks most often?	Ask those students to observe the dialogue. Give them time at the end to share what they learned. Or ask them to set a listening goal for themselves before you begin.
2. Are speakers allowed to finish a thought, even if they pause?	Notice the patterns of speech that students employ. Say, "Thanks for giving Carlos time to think." That signals respect and keeps students silent.
3. Do students cut one another off?	I have no trouble moving in and saying, "Hold, on, Bette, just let Lois finish her whole thought and then you can go. Thank you."
4. Do students address one another by name? Do they make eye contact with the speaker? (In Western cultures it is a sign of respect to acknowledge a speaker by looking at him or her and by using his name.)	Fold index cards horizontally and ask students to write their first name on each side. Display on desks. This helps remind students to use one another's names.

Think about the kinds of questions you ask and how they are posed.

Dialogue Welcomes All Voices

Fourth graders at the Fox Meadow School sat in a circle with the text in front of them. The text was two figures—composites of animals—that I had in my files.

"There are many plants and animals in the rain forest that haven't yet been seen or studied. When botanists or zoologists find a new species they might photograph it or draw it in order to talk to their colleagues about it. Would you pretend that the two animals on your paper are two that were recently discovered in the rain forest in Belize? Which one do you think is the better climber?"

A long wait. Students seemed to be intently studying the drawings. Finally I saw several hands go up. I waited a little longer until more students volunteered.

"I think the one on the right, because it has feet that look like they have little pins on them. That would definitely help them stick into the bark of trees," said Chen who is a child that never volunteers in class. He performs well on written tasks, but he hasn't yet spoken during any discussions.

Brian says, "I can see your point, Chen, but look at the things coming from its head. They look like feathers to me. They could really get stuck in the branches."

"I agree with you, Brian. I think the feathery things would stop it from being a good climber."

"Wait a minute. Look at the feet of the other one—the one on the left. Maybe he's got little suction things under his feet. That would really keep him on the side of a tree." This was from Darlene, who was still struggling to become a fluent reader. Her poor skills often prevented her from performing in public.

"But what about his tail? The left one's got a tail that curls around itself like a snail. It could never last in a tree."

I asked another question: "Can your examples support the idea that form follows function?"

Four students were able to move to this more abstract idea. I encouraged them to carefully unravel the phrase and to give examples from the text as well as from their own experiences. The remaining students continued to critically examine each part of the two animals.

There was no "right" answer, no matter which direction the dialogue headed. I was free to listen to each student as he or she used inquiry and reflection to make meaning.

The dialogue process encouraged the fourth graders to try out their ideas in public. As each participant came to know that his opinion would be treated with respect, I noticed an even greater attempt at risk-taking.

Dialogue Promotes Openness and Trust As The Rule Rather Than As The Exception

Sue Schneider was concerned. It was already March and her third graders were not making the progress in writing that she expected. She wondered if we could engage in dialogue with her kids around the idea of "good" writing. I volunteered to facilitate and we would listen for students' assumptions about good writing. This would help us understand how to proceed. I wanted to encourage the students to feel open to new ideas, to feel comfortable thinking out loud, and to trust that Sue and I would support them in their follow-up efforts.

The next morning I handed everyone two pages. "Each page contains a story written by a third grader in another school," I explained. I asked for volunteers to read

"Cutie the Cat" and "My 1,000 Cars."

"Which story do you think is the better one and why?" I asked.

"Definitely 'Cutie the Cat.'" Nicole was sure about her choice, but she wasn't so sure about her reasons. Her answer was a beginning. I asked questions to help enlarge her thinking.

"What was one thing you noticed about 'Cutie the Cat' that you didn't see in the other story?"

I noticed that Nicole had a confused look on her face. I wanted to find a safe way for her to listen. I turned to the rest of the circle. "Anybody can help her. This is a hard question." Nicole seemed relieved and looked around for support.

"'Cutie' has more words?" Betsy's answer was really a question.

"What do the words do?" I asked for more information.

"They tell about Cutie or the vet who took care of her."

I went to the board. "So are you saying, Betsy, that the author of 'Cutie' uses words to describe things?"

As the dialogue proceeded, I used the students' examples to create the language for good writing. My goal was not to elicit the answers that I wanted the students to "get." Mine was an honest attempt to find out what the students knew about the qualities of writing and about how they might describe writing that is "good."

"I think that 'My 1,000 Cars' is a better story, because 'Cutie' has a sad ending. I didn't like the story, so I vote for the first one."

"Are you saying that one of the qualities of good writing for you is that it has a happy ending?" I asked

"Yes."

"I don't agree with you, Phillip. Sometimes stories can have a sad ending and still be good."

"I don't know any, so I don't think you're right."

"What about 'To Hell With Dying'? The guy dies at the end. That was sad, but it was still a good story."

Phillip was silent. Maybe he was willing to entertain another point of view. "Do you want to think about this for a bit, Phillip, and I'll get back to you later?" I ask this because I want Phillip to understand that I am asking him to seriously consider examining his initial assumption. In a trusting environment, Phillip will know that he is free to change his mind or to stay with his original idea. I will not forget to call on him again before the dialogue has ended.

> **Trust begins in the classroom when I act in a trustworthy manner. Trust continues when members of the classroom behave the same way.**

We moved from dialogue to discussion to writing an action plan. "Choose as your personal goal one of the six criteria that we decided makes writing 'good.' Write it in your journal so that you won't forget. I'll look at them later today," Sue promised,

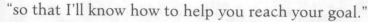

"so that I'll know how to help you reach your goal."

After class, Sue and I looked at each of the journal entries. We spoke about how to create flexible groups to accommodate students with similar goals. We looked for examples of writing that highlighted each goal and spoke about mini-lessons that would help focus the groups. Sue wanted her students to know that their willingness to speak openly in the dialogue gave her the information to help each one work toward achieving his or her writing goal.

Here is how Sue Schneider modeled values of the caring classroom:

❇ She empowered students to set criteria for quality work.

❇ She trusted her students to know what they needed in order to become better writers.

❇ She accepted the challenge to teach what the students set as their goals.

> **When we care we accept the responsibility to work to the best of our ability.**

Dialogue as a Teaching Strategy

Principles of Dialogue

1. All students are encouraged to participate.

2. Questions are posed so that there can be more than one correct response.

3. Students' responses—rather than teachers' desire to cover the material— are the basis for deepening and furthering the dialogue.

4. Questions are challenging but not threatening

Consider Incorporating These Principles into Other Areas:

❇ **During Class Meetings.** Before you create a plan of action or try to find solutions to problems, use dialogues to create empathy for others. Ask students to speak as if they supported the opposing point. Watch for "red flag" words such as all, everyone, boys (as in, "Boys like to play baseball more than girls, so we should be allowed to use the upper playground every day." I might ask, "Do you mean *all* boys? Are you saying that *no* girls like to play baseball?")

❇ **After Read Alouds.** Try not to ask about plot summary, setting, tone, or other concepts that are better covered during your regular reading time. Instead focus on larger themes than can be unfolded slowly and deliberately. Think about themes of care that you are working with: honesty, courage, integrity, compassion. Encourage students to become more precise in their language. Help them to take responsibility for what they say and how they say it.

❃ When you wish to **_examine the historical documents_** that define American culture, talks using the following texts will encourage students to discuss the ideas of justice, liberty, freedom, equality, and fairness. Try juxtaposing parts of each document below with speeches by Native Americans, texts by early Greeks, or editorials in your local newspaper.

> Pledge of Allegiance
> Declaration of Independence
> Bill of Rights
> Gettysburg Address

Action Plan: What Can I Do Today?

Consider active listening as a personal activity. Try taping one of your lessons. Listen for assumptions, beliefs, and values that you may have kept hidden from yourself.

Consider this:

❃ When you facilitate group dialogue do you expect to learn from your students? Can they tell?

❃ What feelings and internal self-talk arise as the dialogue progresses?

❃ Where are you listening from: Your heart? Your mind? Your soul?

❃ What are the silences between the words telling you?

❃ Can you quiet your own mind in order to watch and listen to others?

CHAPTER FIVE

Managing the Caring Classroom

Most children come to school *prepared to learn* and the teachers I know believe that a majority of their students practice responsible behavior every day. They know that most children want to be part of an involved community, because each of us needs to fulfill our sense of belonging to something larger than ourselves. When we feel that we belong to a community we are more likely to be committed to its values. Many of our students—otherwise unmotivated—will do good work because they want to be recognized as a member of the classroom community. They want to please us more than they want to misbehave.

When one walks into a classroom that functions smoothly, where students are actively engaged and involved, it is almost impossible to discover the system the teacher uses. In fact, it often looks as if the classroom is running by itself! We have noted throughout this book that managing behavior is not an isolated learning task. Instead, it is intertwined with curriculum, instructional strategies, satisfying relationships, and the classroom environment. If we attempt to manage children without taking their needs into consideration, we ask them to do things without considering their need for feeling valued, for feeling autonomous, or for believing that they belong to a community that is concerned for them.

Questions to Guide Your Thinking About Managing the Caring Classroom

1. *Do your students understand that the caring classroom is guided by a set of underlying principles?* They must be able to articulate the connection between these principles and the resulting action. Students who are valued are asked how they can work together with the teacher to solve a problem in the classroom.

2. *Do you teach the behavioral skills that contribute to a caring community through direct instruction?* We must help students name the social behaviors essential for the maintenance of such a classroom, teach them the skills for mastery, and assess the results. Students who successfully master skills of concern and responsibility are better able to build on this success. For example, children can learn not to interrupt while another is speaking.

3. *Can your students "find" themselves reflected in the curriculum?* The curriculum must be fluid, evolving, and engaging so that it provides both a window and a mirror for all students. The prosocial values that we wish to stress are continually reinforced through all areas of the curriculum.

4. *Do your students feel that they are respected and valued members of the classroom?* Students who are able to exercise self-determination have a higher degree of self-confidence. When they believe that they have choices and are trusted to make those choices, they feel better about themselves and are able to demonstrate that self-esteem through all that they do.

5. *Are the students aware that when they are unwilling to follow the class's guidelines for behavior, consequences will follow?* The value of being a member of a caring community must appear greater to students than the value of ignoring those guidelines.

When teaching the skills of prosocial behavior, help students take responsibility for their actions, learn from their mistakes, and plan for future behavior. This is not an easy task. It takes time to learn to teach in this manner, and it takes time to see the fruits of our efforts. That is why we must really believe that teaching these skills is doable, worthwhile, and rewarding in the long run. The additional benefits of learning to solve problems collaboratively will serve the students well. They will learn how to reason logically, analyze information, and evaluate their decisions. If you make the time to create community you won't have to use more time to repeat the same information again and again.

The Trouble with Discipline

One of my favorite Mother's Day gifts was an azure blue T-shirt that my own children—Liz and Jeff—gave to me when they were in elementary school. The bold white letters on the front of the shirt told the whole story: BECAUSE I'M THE MOMMY, THAT'S WHY. We have often laughed about that gift, because there were times when that was the exact phrase I used to end discussions. It always worked—in the short run. However, without building on our relationship and continuing a dialogue about why it was important for my children to do as I asked, there would have been none of the positive long-term results that are evident as my children have grown into responsible and loving adults.

> . . . one of the most thoroughly researched findings in social psychology is that the more you reward someone for doing something, the less interest that person will tend to have in whatever he or she was rewarded to do.
>
> —Alfie Kohn, September 1995, *Educational Leadership*

As a classroom teacher I exercised similar authority on several occasions. But discipline programs that rely on power over students only provide a quick fix. "do-this-because-I-tell-you" is the easiest, most effortless strategy to learn. It offers immediate relief to the teacher and the other students in the class. Over time, however, the do-this-or-else strategy has little long-range effects. It is the teacher who increasingly must exercise her authority over students. The message to students is that they are powerless. They must rely on the teacher's approval to decide right from wrong.

> Discipline divorced from curriculum and instruction suggests that it is separate from anything else that happens in the classroom. Such thinking prevents us from looking at the caring classroom as a system in which the action of one part of the system has an effect on every other part.

Snapshots: What Does Managing A Caring Community Look Like?

Respectful Teachers and Students

Children who are able to form warm relationships with adults are able to see adults as supportive and encouraging. If they see adults as adversaries children will be able to justify their disruptive behavior. Jeremy White found this out when, midway through the year, he realized that many of his fifth graders continued to disrupt classroom activities.

One January morning Jeremy called the class together. "Look," he began. "I'm not sure about what has gone wrong here. It seems that every time I try to bring something new and different into the class you guys want to take me on. Then I end up yelling and punishing you and no one seems very happy after that. Do you think the punishments are working?"

The students were unanimous in telling Jeremy that his punishments were harsh and didn't seem to help anyway.

"We keep doing the same things over again anyway. So what's the point of punishing us?"

"We can tell that you just don't like us."

"You're always telling us: 'Do this. Do that.' Why don't you ask us what we want once in a while?"

Jeremy swallowed hard. "Well, then, what should we do differently?"

To his surprise, the students had plenty of suggestions.

Trusting relationships develop slowly, incident by incident. They build from a sense of believing that each member of the relationship will act in a fair and consistent manner.

When Jeremy asked his students, "What could I do to make it better in this room?" he changed the tone. As first the students made outrageous suggestions, but instead of getting angry Jeremy laughed along with them. Soon they began giving some honest suggestions for improving the classroom climate.

A FRAMEWORK FOR ACTIVE LISTENING

* Ask questions instead of making statements.

* Repeat or clarify students' statements to make certain you understand.

* Do not use listening time to "teach" a lesson or to make your point.

* Keep your tone of voice free from sarcasm.

* Thank students for contributing.

"Talk nicer to us."

"Slow down. Sometimes we can't understand what you're saying. You talk too fast."

"When we've got personal problems give us some room."

"Don't make so many rules."

Eventually, the students and Jeremy came to discuss what should be expected of each of them. "If I do this, will you do this," Jeremy seemed to ask. His goal was to eliminate the many rules—mostly unwritten—by which he ran his classroom. He chose to focus on building better relationships with his students. He did this by concencentrating on his behavior as well as his students'. He continued to ask them how they were all doing. He worked to show them that he valued their opinions. Jeremy was eventually able to repair a disruptive classroom and encourage a positive commitment to community ideals.

Self-Disciplined Students

Robin's third graders had trouble getting into their seats quietly and efficiently when they returned from recess. Robin called a class meeting. "Here's my concern," she told them. "It's taking a long time to get into your seats after lunch. This creates a problem, because I seem to be the only one who notices, and I feel as if I'm always yelling. The other problem is that coming in noisy and late also distracts those of you who really are ready to begin to work. Do you think it's a problem too?" When the children agreed, she asked "How long do you think it's taking to sit down?" The children made guesses and decided to time themselves during the coming week.

For the next class meeting Josh presented the results of his timekeeping. The students were surprised to see a visual representation of their guesses. They were further encouraged to find ways to solve their problem.

Karrie made a suggestion that the class immediately chose: "Give us a few minutes to talk and then turn the light off. That will be the signal for us all to return to our seats." Robin reported that three weeks later the students are still able to honor their commitment.

Responsible Decision Making

Autonomous behavior is the distinguishing characteristic of the caring classroom. Students who believe that they are involved in the choices that create their community are more likely to be invested in maintaining that community. While most of us make sure that we give students choices, most of us control the list of choices.

Brenda Pilts teaches second grade in a large city in the West. She noticed that class meetings, held the first half hour of the day, were an effective way to begin the process of responsible decision making. The students demonstrated respectful listening, consensus building, and active engagement in the process. Brenda was dismayed to note that there was little carryover into the rest of the day. When the meeting was over, the students reverted back to conventional behavior.

"First I asked myself what I was doing to contribute to the situation," she reflected. "Then I began to think of ways to help my students transfer the skills they learned during class meetings to the rest of the school day."

EXTENDING CARING FROM CLASS MEETING TO THE REST OF THE DAY

✻ *Do I think my students are too young to handle responsibility?* Six year olds can suggest the agenda for each day's class meeting. Third graders can brainstorm alternative learning experiences when they have competed their assigned work. Fifth graders can decide how best to complete several weeklong assignments by proposing a personal educational plan. In each case, teachers can probably complete the task more quickly, more neatly, or more efficiently. But if you want students to become more responsible in their decision making, they must have real decisions to make.

✻ *Do I worry that my students and their parents will think I'm too permissive?* Do not confuse progressive with permissive. Seldom do we increase a student's ability to make responsible decisions by flattering them, by rewarding them for choosing what we wanted them to chose in the first place, or by giving them insignificant decisions to make. Students and parents must see that the decisions they make are significant to the creation and maintenance of a rigorous and intellectually challenging community.

✻ *Am I afraid I do not have the time to spend teaching these skills because I have so much curriculum to cover?* Community building is at the heart of school improvement. Without community there is no commitment to respecting each other or to learning. If we increasingly find students who do not share the values of the caring community we have little choice but to include these skills as part of our curriculum. It is essential to think of curriculum as more than the content of the material students must learn. We must widen our concept of curriculum to include the skills and behaviors that are necessary to support the mastery of content.

Start With One Skill. Brenda set out, in small steps, to help students make the transfer. First, she identified one skill that she wanted to see transferred. Then she tried to help students find ways to recognize that they were demonstrating that skill in other ways.

"I'd like to ask your help in solving a problem I have." Brenda was sincere about asking students for help in solving her problem. She told them that she did not think she could solve the problem alone, and since they were also members of the community, they should have a right to help out with her problem. "I am always so pleased to know that you can make responsible decisions when we are in class meetings, but

I have noticed that when you are stuck with a problem during the rest of the day, you ask me first. Do you think that's right?"

"How do you think that makes me feel?" Brenda asked the students to put themselves in her place. Empathy is a difficult skill for young children to demonstrate, but it is one that is worthwhile to pursue. Empathetic understanding is the basis for resolving conflict as well as tolerating an open-minded consideration of others' ideas.

"What could we do to solve my problem?" The key word is *we*. It implies that both Brenda and the students will assume responsibility for new behaviors. ("If I do this . . .will you do this?")

Family Involvement

We must remember that students in an empathy-oriented community are more willing to respect that community if there is consistency between home and school. Parents whose prior experience with school is either negative or minimal may need more encouragement to build a home-school connection. Parents who feel included and encouraged are more apt to recognize the value of building relationships with other students, teachers, and with one another.

The Pollution Solution Club at the Post Road Elementary School in White Plains, New York, sponsored a beach cleanup day one Saturday in March. The PTA provided buses to take parents and their children to the beach at Croton Point Park where they spent the day picking up trash and other garbage that washed up during the winter. At lunchtime everyone met in the lodge to share a warm lunch provided by several mothers, fathers, and students.

This community activity was significant for several reasons:

- ✳ **All Together Now.** Buses encouraged all parents and children to stay together. Automobiles would have kept them isolated. Buses also provided the means for many parents—who otherwise had no way to get to the beach—with transportation. Finally, buses did not separate those who had alternative transportation from those who did not.

- ✳ **Parents See for Themselves.** Parents were involved in an authentic activity that the children took very seriously. They did not have to be told that the youngsters worked cooperatively and vigorously to clean the beach; they were there to see it and to help in the process.

- ❋ **The Real Thing.** Students were able to demonstrate responsible decision making, respect for all opinions, and concern for the environment in a real context. Many children whose achievements in school were seldom honored found another way to feel valued.

- ❋ **Everyone Pitches In.** A caring community was evident as all members shared hard work, worked toward a common good, and broke bread together.

Perhaps It Is Not the Child Who Is "Out Of Line"; Perhaps It Is the System

Video Journal

A fifth grade teacher I know has been able to change her teaching style dramatically over the past three years by keeping a video journal. As painful as it is to see oneself on video, video journals are one of the very best ways to assess our practice.

Benefits

My colleague saw that she seldom smiled. "I thought I was the sweetest teacher in the school. I was shocked to see the grimace on my face!" She also saw that she called on the same three noisy boys much of time, while the quieter students, who respectfully raised their hands, were almost always passed over.

On several occasions she shared the tapes with her students, and she learned that they too were often unaware of their behavior. The video journal proved to be a far more valuable tool in improving the students'—and the teacher's—skills than any verbal description could ever have been.

The tapes also had an unexpected benefit. The students learned that their teacher wanted to improve her own skills and was interested in the comments and support of her class. The video journal helped to demystify the teaching process for both the teacher and students. Can you imagine what that did to improve the students' self-esteem?

Teachers Examine Their Practices

Teachers who take more responsibility for their own role in creating or diminishing the caring classroom reframe the underlying questions that inform their work. "When will *they* stop behaving like babies?" becomes "What can *I* do to begin analyzing their behaviors differently?"

Our teaching habits are based on a set of beliefs and values. We too are part of the system. We must continue to examine our professional selves just as we examine every other part of the big picture.

Disillusionment in One School

In a classroom in an inner city school several teachers met to tell me about their experiences in managing a caring classroom. Beverly was the first to speak. "Remember when we first started this school? Remember how idealistic we were? We were going to love these kids to death. We were going to make up for all of the poverty and the low self-esteem they came to us with.

Marvella, remember how we used to come in here midway through that year and the whole next year mad as could be?"

Marvella was quick to answer. "Remember? Do you think I could forget how many days I was ready to end it all? I couldn't believe those ungrateful kids didn't love us for all that we were doing for them. I couldn't figure out why their attitude was worse than when we began the school." Among their complaints, the teachers listed students who never completed homework, those who seldom finished the work they had begun, and the language students used when speaking to the staff and to one another.

The teachers formed a supportive group to talk about these experiences. When they first discovered that the students were acting out more and more frequently, the teachers first blamed the students. They speculated that the student really didn't want to learn anything, that they were "too far gone." Some days they saw it as parents' fault. Other times they decided that it was the media's fault or that society was the culprit.

In time, Marvella suggested that they look more closely at their own behavior. It began to dawn on them that what *they* saw as loving behavior, their students saw as lack of caring. When they forgave students who didn't complete homework because "I was up all night taking care of my little brother," students saw this as a teacher who didn't care enough. When they gave the class chance after chance to behave without imposing any consequences, the kids saw them as easy marks.

"We were loving these kids to death. We were smothering them with our love." Tyrone Elliot spoke now for the whole group. "We finally had to sit down with the kids and ask them what they saw in us and what they needed from us."

Humbling, perhaps, but it turned out to be an opportunity for insight on teaching and learning. When the group was able to depersonalize the experience, they could examine the events more objectively. Together teacher and students worked toward understanding each others' motives and expectations. The students no longer felt that they were being denied access to the teachers' knowledge and authority. The teachers learned to say what they meant directly and explicitly.

Fair Is Not Always Equal

Treating everyone in your class fairly does not always mean treating them in exactly the same way. When we know that students act out for a variety of reasons we are in a better position to decide how best to handle the situation. This takes time and practice because in order to make the hundreds of decisions we are called upon to respond to, we have to internalize an entire menu of strategies.

Strategies for Intervention

Steps to Teaching Students Problem-Solving Skills

Students are more likely to use the steps suggested to solve their problems if we provide them with ample opportunities to learn, practice, and talk about the results. It is important to be consistent and to use classroom examples as teaching opportunities. At first you will probably want to stop several times each day and remind students to use the steps to solve their problems. Over time—if you are clear about letting students know that you expect them to solve their own problems using the steps—you will notice that your students will seldom need you to intervene.

WHEN CHILDREN ACT OUT, ASK YOURSELF:

1. Is the student misbehaving because he or she is bored? Do you need to examine the curriculum or the instructional strategies you are employing so that students can find validation and success in the work?

2. Is the student acting out or cutting up because she is afraid of being "found out"? Many students with weak skills are embarrassed or ashamed of the fact that their abilities are below those of other students. These feelings are often masked by bravado or an I-don't-care attitude. In fact, they do care.

3. Is the student off-task because he doesn't understand the directions? Many students would rather do anything but admit that they didn't understand or don't know how to do the assignment. This is especially true if he fears others will laugh at him; if the teacher scolds him for not paying attention in the first place; or if he has met repeated failure in school.

4. Does the student know which skills and understandings are necessary for demonstrating the prosocial behaviors that are valued? We must assume that unless the skills of respect, responsibility, kindness, and concern for others have been taught directly and continually assessed, they have not been learned.

5. Are my expectations for this student reasonable? Do I recognize the differences in our cultures, and do I act with respectful understanding of those differences? Are my expectations developmentally appropriate?

6. Am I taking this too personally? Is the student challenging other students or my authority? Can I avoid being sucked in to the power struggle?

STEPS

1. *Name the Problem.* Let each person have a turn to state the problem as he or she sees it. Students will learn that there are many versions of the truth.

2. *List Several Solutions.* Students will learn that there may be several alternatives to any problem and that they do have choices.

3. *Explain Consequences.* How does each choice affect each person involved? Students will learn that for every action there is a consequence for everyone.

4. *Consider Consensus.* What choice is the most fair to everyone? Students will learn that solutions that are arrived at through consensus are win-win.

By teaching your students steps to solve their own problems in authentic situations you provide them with the knowledge and the tools to manage their own behavior. Patty Dempsey, the teacher in chapter one, talked about the changes that have resulted in her first grade class. "This year my students have just as many problems as they always seem to have. What's different is that now they are able to solve most of them by themselves."

Social Contracts

Social contracts are agreements between teachers and students about the rules and consequences for classroom behavior. The goal, of course, is to work with students to develop clear and explicit behavior guidelines and consequences that are fairly and consistently employed. Writing social contracts with students can help prevent problems before they occur.

The most effective contracts are developed when students are part of the process. The act of discussing behavior guidelines and expectations as a class is even more important than what the rules are. In fact, we would do well to question our own beliefs about controls and limits as we invite students to partake in the process.

The Following Guidelines Will Help You Write Social Contracts:

* *Teach Meaning of Behavior Guidelines.* Be sure students understand what the guidelines mean. Terms like *responsibility* and *concern* are abstract concepts for many students. When we ask students to "show respect for one another, for school property, and the community," we must make certain that the principle of respect is translated into concrete examples. What does respect look like? What does it sound like?

* *Make Consequences Clear.* Students who are involved in determining consequences are on their way to taking responsibility—not only for their actions—but also for the results of those actions.

❋ *Teach Reasons for Rules.* In establishing rules, help students see that rules are not necessary when respect, responsibility, and kindness are evident in the classroom. Enforcing rules through consequences is the alternative a community resorts to when its members have not yet found ways to have their needs met.

Consequences Vs. Punishments

How Do They Differ?

Consequences are simple and direct. They are related to the rules in a logical and instructive way. Consequences preserve the child's dignity while assuming that she would do better if she could. An appropriate consequence for a student who shouts out during a discussion might be to write her next response on paper or to wait several minutes before speaking again. A punishment, by contrast, might be to send the student to the principal's office where "she can think about her behavior."

Resorting to severe punishments such as sending a student to the principal's office may help in the short term, but they seldom confront the real problem. Unless we work together to address how we can help the student get his or her needs met in an appropriate way, it will remain our responsibility to become a policeman to that student.

MS. YOUNG'S FIRST GRADE EXAMPLE

Eleanora Young teaches first grade in a small town near Philadelphia. She and her students developed these consequences during class meetings to solve problems that developed throughout the school year.

Problem	Consequences
Noisy during assemblies	Practice walking, sitting in the auditorium
	Rearrange seating
	Stay back from the assembly
Talking when others are speaking	Five minutes of no talking
	Go to time-out area
	Go to time-out in a buddy-teacher's room
Hitting or bullying others	Private "tutoring" after school to learn and practice alternative skills
	Social contract with student, parents, principal

Writing A Social Contract With Second Graders

When budget cuts signaled larger class sizes, Jodi Lesse realized that she would be spending much of her day serving as a referee for her thirty-eight second graders. She decided to begin the year working on developing a social contract with her students. Unless they put something in writing Judy knew that the responsibility for keeping the class under control would be hers alone. Besides, she was tired of hearing second graders tell her that nothing she did was ever *fair*!

Kindness Above All

Jodi Lesse began the first week developing a contract with the class. The first principle she introduced was kindness. The students shared ways others had been kind to them and how they had been kind to others. She chose books to read to the students, such as Eve Bunting's *The Wednesday Surprise*, in which kindness could be discussed as a group. When she created cooperative-learning activities, kindness was the value stressed and written about on T-charts. ("What does kindness look like? What does it sound like?")

Then, Jodi and her students used class meeting time to develop the guidelines for behavior as well as the consequences of not following them. This was a difficult task that required a lot of discussion and negotiation.

Here is what Jodi displayed in her second grade classroom:

WE WILL INCLUDE ANYONE IN A GAME WHO WANTS TO PLAY

Consequences:
1. Sit under the tree.
2. The game will end.
3. The whole class will come inside to talk about the problem.

Paley Said It Well

Vivian Paley's book, *You Can't Say You Can't Play,* (Harvard University Press, 1992) had a profound effect on Jodi. In that book, Paley, a kindergarten teacher, employed a unique strategy to probe dimensions of morality. She held conversations with students throughout her K-5 school, asking for their comments on what would happen in schools if children were told that they could not say to another child, "you cannot play." Jodi used Paley's story to describe a caring classroom for her second graders.

"Should one child be allowed to keep another child from joining a group?" Paley asked her students. They discussed the question. Then Jodi said to her class, " What if we created this rule for ourselves: 'You can't say you can't play.'" Jodi wasn't sure how her students would receive the idea of including everyone in all play groups. She did know that this would be a long and involved discussion. She knew that it was not enforceable unless her students understood the reason for the rule and were willing to become personally responsible for carrying it out. In the end Jodi was pleased that she spent the time talking about such an important issue.

An Entire School Creates Rules and Consequences

Anna James and her faculty at the Edgerton School in New London, Connecticut, have developed five school-wide rules. At this first attempt with a school-wide initiative, students were not included in the initial planning. However, the results of the Edgerton faculty were significant for several reasons. Their rules were meant to provide students with principles for acting. They were not prescriptions which often limit dialogue and focus narrowly on school behavior rather than on lifelong social values. The rules were printed on large sheets of oak tag and visible everywhere: In every classroom, in the main office, the teachers' lounge, and in the hallways and auditorium. They served as constant visual reminders that this caring community shared common expectations, common language, and common consequences.

Rules for Enjoying Edgerton

Be safe and keep others safe.
Be respectful of yourself and others.
Be a good learner and listener.
Be responsible.
Be honest.

Consequences for Breaking Rules

LEVELS

1. *Reminder.* Teacher reminds student about inappropriate behavior in the classroom, referring to one of the rules listed above.

2. *Time-Out Somewhere in the Classroom,* during which student reflects on behavior and regains self-control.

3. *Time-Out in Another Classroom.* Used mainly when students continues to misbehave in his or her own classroom. Students stays in another "buddy" classroom to reflect and regain self-control. Student will return to regular classroom when ready to follow rules. Parent will be notified by teacher when this step is necessary.

4. *Time-Out with Principal.* Student will be sent to the principal to discuss rule-breaking behavior. Principal will call parent or guardian.

5. *Suspension/Parent in Classroom.* This will be used at the principal's discretion for severe or frequent breaking of the rules by the student. The student will be suspended and the required schoolwork will be done at home, or the parent or guardian will accompany the student to class for the entire day.

The rules and their consequences were translated into Spanish and included in the handbook that was sent home to all parents. Crucial to the understanding of the rules as effective teaching tools was a parent-student response form that was meant to be signed and dated by students and their parents or guardians: "We have read and discussed the 'school-wide rules and consequences' section of the Edgerton handbook. We will do our part to support efforts to make Edgerton a safe, productive, and enjoyable place to learn."

What If All Else Fails?

There is an expectation that all children will grow a year in a year's time. If they do not, we are often compelled to pass them to the next class anyway. Social pressure, cost factors, and limited alternatives conspire against taking the time to help all students reach their maximum level of achievement. No matter how scrupulous we are in monitoring our own behavior, in learning new instructional strategies, and in creating student-centered curricula, there are some children who have not yet mastered the social skills or the understanding necessary for self-control.

Students' Reputations Precede Them

The reputation of these children often precedes them, as in: "Wait until you get Billy in your class. What a handful." "Everyone knows the whole third grade is the worst ever. If you're thinking of retiring, this would be the year!" Threats and punishments to such students do not seem to help. In fact, punishments often make these students heroes to their friends who see the child as tough enough to take whatever the school can dish out. The pleasure of misbehaving, therefore, outweighs the fear of getting caught. As more and more responsibility for "catching" him is placed on the teacher, less and less responsibility is felt by the child. You can be relatively sure that children such as these have learned well the value of misbehavior long before they have entered your classroom.

Working It Out

Janine Allison, a teacher at the John F. Kennedy Middle School, and her student, Wayne, seemed to have problems from the first day of school. Wayne constantly disrupted the class, seldom came prepared, and served as the class clown. By early November Janine realized that whatever she tried failed. She finally asked her colleague, Robert Torres, to act as the facilitator in a negotiation process with Wayne.

Facilitator: Wayne, why don't you go first. What do you see as the problem between you and Mrs. A.?

Student: Mrs. A. is prejudiced toward me.

Teacher: That's not true. It's just that I've repeatedly warned you that you will fail my class if you don't start working.

Facilitator: Is that true, Wayne? Have you heard Mrs. A. say that?

Student: I'm not doing anything, because you don't care about me anyway.

Teacher: What would you like me to do to improve things between us?

Student: I want you to call me by my name like you do the other boys. And let me take the attendance to the nurse's office.

Teacher: I'll do that. And I would like you not to call out when I'm talking or to make fun of other students in the class.

Janine Allison was amazed to learn how easily she could comply with Wayne. She never dared to hope that they could create a new relationship in the classroom. Wayne, a sixth grader, had never been taken so seriously by any teacher. He emerged with his dignity intact, knowing that he had direct access to Janine.

When Behavior Problems Don't Go Away

1. *Write an Individual Social Contract.* To ensure success the contract should include clear and explicit expectations, specific tasks for the student, her parents, and the teacher; and a manageable period of time for completion.

2. *Develop a Weekly (or Hourly) Progress Sheet.* After developing at a class meeting a rubric entitled, "what an effective class looks like," ask children to select one item as a goal for themselves the next week. During the following week, children can evaluate their progress by filling in an hourly (at first), then a weekly progress sheet, as shown on page 83.

3. *Create a Time-Out Corner or Room.* Teachers can remind students who continue to interrupt others or who speak out when others are speaking, for example, that the consequence is to spend 5-10 minutes in a time-out room. An alternative is to ask them to go into a colleague's room for time-out. This is only effective, of course, if the student thinks that she's really missing something. If a student spends those ten minutes passing notes and whispering to her friend in the other class, then the learning experience is hardly what we intend!

   Tip: *Do not keep students back from physical education, art, or music class. Not only do we dishonor the professionalism of our colleagues who teach these subjects but we also give the message to our students that those classes are not as important as the ones that we teach.*

4. *Teach Self-Talk.* Most of us talk to ourselves in an attempt to remember the steps of a procedure. ("Let's see. I'm supposed to tie this knot with the left flap over the right.") Why not try to help students use the same strategy to improve their behavior? Demonstrate this technique by thinking out loud as the student observes ("Clara said she doesn't like my

Name _____

PROGRESS SHEET

Appropriate Classroom Behavior:

On Time, Prepared, Respectful, Raise hand to be recognized, Wait your turn to speak, Stay in seat, Walk when entering room, Encourage others, Praise others, Cooperate, Tell the truth, Low voices, Works independently, Keeps work area clean, Polite

Inappropriate Classroom Behavior:

Late without a pass, Unprepared, Interrupt others, Call out, Loud voice, Distracts others (words or gestures), Disrespectful to others, Get out of seat, Uncooperative, Refuse to work with others, Foul language, Put downs, Leave a mess, Takes things without asking, Damage property

Date	Appropriate Behavior	Inappropriate Behavior	Need

shoes. But that doesn't mean she doesn't like me. Anyway, I'm not going to react to her. I'm just going to turn my back and walk away."). Have students practice this technique with you and with peers.

5. ***Institute a Conflict Resolution Program.*** Negative behavior is often the result of an inability to call forth alternative strategies of action. Teachers and students often make matters worse by handling conflicts in destructive ways—or they don't deal with them at all because they are afraid to confront the conflict. The result is often hurt feelings, compromises that are quickly forgotten, or gossip that pits "us" against "them." When students and teachers learn basic negotiation skills they report that they can move from conflict to collaboration.

> **These skills need to be overlearned. The process of negotiation is contrary to our instinctive desire to strike back during a conflict. It takes practice and consistency. And more practice!**

Making Connections

The skills that students learn as they participate in cooperative learning groups, class meetings, and dialogues are many of the same collaborative skills used in managing our own behavior: active listening, developing empathy for another's position, asking for clarification or for more information before drawing conclusions. Students soon learn that they can retain their status and at the same time seek greater understanding of another's needs. We need to help students see that they are already showing caring. Managing in the caring classroom takes time and effort. It involves part art, part science, and part humor. It is part of the entire system of learning and teaching.

Action Plan: What Can I Do Today?

Try a Bulletin Board Experiment

The next time you decide to put up new bulletin boards, think instead about taking everything down from the walls. Leave them empty until your students notice and ask why. Use the empty walls as the entry into a conversation around the purpose of displaying material and whose decision it should be.

Before you begin, ask yourself:

- ❄ Am I willing to negotiate the use of wall space with my students?

- ❄ Can I use this dialogue as an opportunity to teach problem-solving skills? Consensus building? Conflict resolution?

- ❄ How can I help my students transfer these skills into other areas of classroom life?

CHAPTER SIX

Ending the Year with Pride

T he end of the school year is a time to bring closure to the activities and efforts that have helped to make yours a more caring classroom. It is at this time that you and your students can look back at the year that has passed and anticipate the opportunities the future provides. Let's look at the journal entries of some teachers at that point in the school year.

What I Learned About Myself As A Learner

My goal for the day was to listen to a student and look at her or him the entire time she or he was talking. It was amazing. I had to *make* myself focus and not pay attention to any distractions. I chose lunchtime and listened to two boys. They talked on and on and on. It was as if it were a magic time in another world. It made me wonder if anyone had ever given them total attention. Then I thought how rarely any of us is the sole recipient of someone's attention. I valued the time and value these students even more.

—Leslie (Kansas City, Missouri)

[This work] teaches restraint and respect for other viewpoints. Respect fosters love and empowers each of us to be more responsible with our choices. It teaches us to hold back emotion in the pursuit of seriously considering other ideas. . .it's like the scales of justice.

—John (Philadelphia, Pennsylvania)

Leslie and John are two teachers whose journal entries remind us how engaging it is to be a reflective practitioner. Their writing made visible that while their students were learning and growing, they were too. By writing their thoughts, each teacher had tangible evidence of the internal monologue that somehow gets lost in the "doing" of everyday life.

Your Turn

If you have been keeping a journal or trying some of our action plan suggestions, review your notes and set goals for the new year.

"It's Not Over Till It's Over!"

It is worthwhile to revisit an activity that your students completed at the beginning of the year. They can interview each other again or make another class quilt. Seeing a before-and-after-project gives your class a visible representation of how much they have grown.

> **QUESTIONS TO GUIDE YOUR YEAR-END REFLECTION:**
>
> ❋ *Have you noticed any patterns in the way you interact with your students?*
>
> ❋ *Was there one goal that you were proud to have achieved? Could you develop a framework for thinking about how you achieved it?*
>
> ❋ *What do you wish you had done differently? What other choices were available? Which would you choose to focus on next year?*

Mr. Cohen's Second Graders Grow

Start of the Year

During the first month of school Gil Cohen's second graders interviewed each other. They asked such questions as "What is your favorite food?" "How many brothers and sisters do you have?" or "When is your birthday?" Gil was not surprised by the interviews. They were fairly typical of the questions seven year olds ask one another.

Partners then traced each others' hands on construction paper, cut out the tracing, and illustrated the hand with answers to the interview. It was with these "hands" that partners introduced one another to the whole class. The hands were then arranged in a large circle, hand-to-wrist, on the bulletin board. The title of the display was WE ARE UNIFIED.

End of the Year

At the end of the year Gil decided to try the exercise again. He wanted to learn whether his students used skills of cooperation and care. He listened carefully to the interview questions they asked. This time he heard: "What was the kindest thing you did this year?" "What did you learn when we wrote poetry with the grandparents in the nursing home?" and "What was your best homework to do with your mom?"

Now when the students shared what they learned through their interviews, Gil heard them talking about showing respect to other kids and about learning to solve their own problems before asking the teacher. The students also reflected on what the experience told them in September and what it told them in May. He created a second large circle of hands on the bulletin board.

Gil hung the first circle and intertwined it with the second. This time the bulletin board read WE ARE ALL PART OF A CARING CLASSROOM.

Opportunities to Close the Year with Care

1. ***Round-Robin Thanks.*** Students begin with large sheets of newspaper. At the top they write their own names in a decorative manner. At a signal each student passes the sheet to the next person who writes a "thanks for. . ." note to that original student. The newsprint continues to be passed in a clockwise direction, until each page is filled with positive memories of thanks from every member of the class.

2. ***I Will Always Remember You.*** A variation of the above is to post each student's sheet of newsprint on the walls around the room. Everyone is given a packet of self-stick notes. Any time during the week students write notes to one another on the self-stick notes, and affix them to the sheets of newspaper. The messages are always positive and complete the statement, "I will always remember you because. . ."

3. ***Class Poem.*** Groups of students work together to contribute a verse to a class poem. Verses might include memories of class trips, activities that supported learning, and visitors to the class. The class poem can be

published in a final edition of a class or school newspaper, delivered at a final assembly, or framed to be hung in the classroom.

4. *A Magazine for the New Students.* Students publish a magazine filled with their memories of the passing year and advice to the crop of students who will enter in September. The magazine can include interviews and pictures of the year's highlights, as well as anecdotal examples of the social skills that were learned during the year.

5. *True or False?* Students have many questions regarding what life in the next grade will be like, especially when students are moving on to a new school. During "true and "false?" students generate interview questions in order to get a more realistic picture of the next grade. They invite older students to be interviewed on an afternoon toward the end of school. Afterwards, students compare the responses they received with their original perceptions.

6. *Thanks, and More.* Thank-you notes and letters are sent to people who seldom get recognized for their contributions to the caring classroom. Students can work in groups to organize the lists, write the letters, and illustrate them. Recipients can include those who have had actual contact with the students and those who brought pleasure to the students' lives through their acts or deeds. For example, children might write to the TV weatherman for helping them know the forecast for the day (that way children can choose clothing appropriately) or, in one case I observed, to the local highway department who had delayed their work every morning in order to allow the school bus to pass and bring the children to school on time.

HOW MANY OF THESE FOLKS CAN BE THANKED?

❊ *office staff*

❊ *custodians*

❊ *school crossing guards*

❊ *parent volunteers*

❊ *tour guides*

❊ *bus drivers*

❊ *older students*

❊ *book authors, illustrators*

Teacher as Cheerleader

Now that your students feel like valued members of a caring community, you will want to spend some time celebrating your success. Take time from your hectic end-of-the year schedule to reflect on your collective accomplishments. As a cheerleader, you serve to honor the good intentions of all students and to model ways to value success.

Help Students See The Best In Themselves

Name the Skills Learned

Last May, Diane Ruggerio helped her class list the skills they mastered during the year. They named the knowledge skills: "We learned how to subtract three-place numbers. . ." "We learned how ice can crack rocks. . ." "We read four chapter books."

And they listed social skills: "We learned to make decisions through consensus. . ." "We practiced showing respect for the environment and for each other. . ."

They listed their trips: "We went to the kindergarten to read the books we wrote." "We walked to the park to clean it for Earth Day. . ." They named the visitors who came into their classroom. They recalled the assembly programs and the special luncheon the cafeteria workers prepared in celebration of the one hundredth day of school.

Diane taped their lists to the walls. The students could hardly believe how much they had accomplished during the year. "I couldn't believe it myself," Diane told me later. "I guess I get so caught up with the daily routine that I never really stopped to celebrate how much these kids have done."

Take It Further

Extend your focus on the positive by asking students to:

❋ Write about what they learned from looking at the lists.

❋ Choose one of the skills that was the most difficult for you and tell how you mastered it.

❋ Discuss where they should go from here.

Teach Students How To "Pass It On"

End-of-Year Experiences in a Grade Four Class

As we pointed out earlier, one final responsibility your class might undertake is to pass along information to next year's class. As the "cheerleader" you help students recall activities or ideas that they thought were especially helpful in creating their caring community.

Warren, a fourth grade teacher, tried just that—and it was quite an eye-opener for him.

A few days before school ended he began to dismantle the classroom just as he had done every June. This time, though, he asked himself why he was doing this and who it would serve.

Questions His Own Routines

He knew that he removed the papers, posters, and projects from around the room to return them to the students. What would his class think if he asked them to decorate the big bulletin board on the side wall for the incoming fourth graders?

Most students loved the idea. "We could say 'welcome' to the new kids and tell them what they are going to do in fourth grade," Eliot told him.

"They'd probably like to see a bulletin board that kids made for them."

"We could say what we thought fourth grade was going to be like and what it was really like."

"I agree with you, Kenny. We could figure out what could scare kids about the next grade and tell them not to be afraid. We could tell them it's going to be okay."

The discussion continued until the students broke into groups to design and execute bulletin boards that would be in place the first day of the new term. Warren got permission from the custodians to cover the children's work with newspapers during the summer so that it would not interfere with their cleaning schedule.

Benefits

Warren wondered why he always assumed full responsibility for displaying that first bulletin board. This year-end activity had the potential to give his present class an opportunity to reflect on their year as well as to serve as mentors to others. And surely new students would especially wish to be welcomed by their peers.

So much of what we do we have always done, and that's why it's not easy to question our practices. Change for its own sake is not the issue. Rather, it is to continue to reflect on what we do and to ask whether it contributes to a classroom community or care and empathy.

OTHER GREAT ACTIVITIES

✳ *Make a Video of Your Students Welcoming the New Class.* Each group might describe part of the daily routine or talk about the value of class meetings, dialogues, or resolving conflicts peacefully.

✳ *Publish a Newspaper for the Next Class.* Your class might want to include an advice column, an interview with you, and photos or artwork that evoke memories of projects that served the school or community.

✳ *Invite Parents and Other Interested Community Members to a Final Town Meeting* (a larger variation of your class meeting). Students can set the agenda to include a review of the year as well as recommendations for schoolwide or community projects that need to be initiated or continued.

Use Literature To Say Good-Bye

Moving On

Many of us approach the end of the year with bittersweet feelings. Just as we feel connected and part of the community we have worked so hard to build, we must let it all go. Some teachers have delayed these feeling by looping students—teaching them for more than one year, or working with a group of students and colleagues for a period of several years.

Students too may experience signs of distress at the end of the year. Emotions range from pure euphoria to acting-out behavior not seen since early in the term. You can be the cheerleader even when children are sad. When you read aloud at this time of the year, focus on the range of feelings that are available to all of us. It is the ability to experience all of the human emotions that helps to develop sympathetic understanding for one another.

BOOKS THAT FOCUS ON SEPARATION, INDEPENDENCE, AND DEVELOPING COMPETENCIES

Alan Arkin. *The Lemming Condition*. (1976). New York: Harper and Row

Byrd Baylor. *I'm in Charge of Celebrations*. (1986). New York: Scribner's

Barbara Brenner. *Wagon Wheels*. (1978). New York: Harper and Row

Eleanor Coerr. *The Josefina Story Quilt*. (1986). New York: Harper and Row

John Reynolds Gardiner. *Stone Fox*. (1983). New York: Harper Trophy

Jamaica Kincaid. *Annie John*. (1986). New York: Farrar, Straus, and Giroux

When Parents Have Been Partners

You have observed how much more supportive they are since you included them in your goals for building the caring community. As the year ends, you can continue the tradition of keeping parents well informed.

Portfolio Night

The end of the year is a wonderful opportunity for students and their parents to review the year's work. In Joyce White's class parents are invited to a portfolio night in which the family group sits to review the contents of the students' portfolios. This is clearly the students' program. It is the child who informs her parents of the growth that she has made during the year.

For example, Janella Lou Brown and her father sat at a table in the corner of her fifth grade classroom. Both of them knew that Joyce White—Janella Lou's teacher—was in sight and would be available to clarify any questions that might arise, but it would be Janella Lou who would explain the contents of the portfolio to Mr. Brown.

Janella Lou carefully removed five pieces of writing that she wanted to talk about. She also found the fifth grade rubric for good writing. "Look at this, Pop. See, in the beginning of the year I only wrote about one or two paragraphs. As the year went on, my stories got longer, because I learned how to put more details in my work. I tried to use more colorful language and to 'tell, not show' like Mrs. White says."

Janella Lou's dad took his time to read through the five stories. He occasionally looked at the rubric and then back at the stories. Before he could finish Janella Lou began again. "And look, here, Pop." She pointed to the third paper. "By this time I really started to use punctuation marks, especially exclamation marks. See how I never used them in September and October?"

When they finished the stories Janella Lou found examples of problem-solving in math and science to show her dad. Again, she produced a rubric that indicated levels of elaboration and critical thinking. Mr. Brown asked her to tell him why she had to write out or draw the way she solved each problem. "To me, math means you either know the right answer or you don't. Period," he told her.

"We learned that if you can't tell how you got it, you really don't understand it," Janella Lou told him. Before she could finish, Joyce White was at her side to explain the reason students are being asked to write how they solved math problems. This was an excellent opportunity to educate Mr. Brown and to support Janella Lou's educational growth.

Portfolio night ended with apple juice and brownies and a chance for father and daughter to look around the room at evidence of the caring classroom. Joyce White, who had to be sold on the value of such a night, expressed satisfaction that the goals of the evening had been met tenfold. "Many of these parents used to come in only when their kids were in trouble," she told me. "But tonight they had a chance to see the progress their kids made. They were so proud; some of these parents hardly ever get to see their children as academics."

Parents As Teachers

Ms. Lee Tackles Problem Head-On

In late May, Dorothy Lee began to notice that many of her fourth grade girls became more quiet during class discussions, took less risks in cooperative groups, and deferred more to the boys on the playground. Lee was aware of the literature that described such phenomena, which indicated that boys and girls respond differently in the classroom, with some girls feeling unsafe and hesitating before responding for fear of being teased. (Although, I should add, there is as much variation *among* girls as there is *among boys and girls*).

Holding a Panel

Dorothy invited five women—parents and community members—to present a panel discussion about how each triumphed over obstacles. She deliberately invited women not only to help her girls identify with role models, but also to help her boys value the role of women in society. She hoped the class would learn from the parent-teachers and that her students might gain the strength to grow beyond their present behavior.

The panel was brilliant. A first grade teacher who taught many of the students talked about how she overcame childhood polio and entered college to become a teacher—even though she was discouraged from getting a teaching position because of her handicap. A nurse-practitioner told the students how she was discouraged from becoming a doctor because she was a girl, and how she was planning on entering medical school anyway; she had saved the money by working in another profession.

A beauty-parlor owner discussed how she sometimes believed that her job wasn't important until she realized how good it felt to make women feel beautiful. She finally decided that she would no longer value success by any standard but her own. "Am I doing good things for people? Are they happier after they see me than before? If I can honestly say 'yes' then I feel successful."

The last to speak was the head of the school district's athletic department. She talked about feeling excluded by boys as a child, when she wanted to play their games. She decided that her life's work would be to help others avoid going through the same humiliation and frustration. She urged the girls in the class to stay involved in sports and to think about becoming professional athletes or referees. She also asked the boys in the room to think about what it might feel like to exclude others from playing. "If winning weren't everything, what would games look like?" she asked.

Program Continues

The second part of the program was just as powerful. The students were encouraged to ask questions of the panel members. The class spent many months in the beginning of the year learning interview techniques. But Dorothy was unprepared for the depth of questions, in particular, from the girls. She was excited with the range of questions and the seriousness with which the students took their responsibility to learn.

Unexpected Results

"The panel was one of the best gifts I gave my students all year," she told me. "First of all, I realized that I didn't have to do all the teaching by myself. What a relief to know that there are parents and other community members who can teach my kids. Secondly, I think the students learned so much today because these women were so real. And I know the women felt honored to have shared their stories with the class. I'd do this again in a minute!"

Students are more prepared to make connections between home and school when their family's culture is acknowledged and validated. These students are better able to feel that they belong to a caring classroom community, and ultimately to be more responsible members of our larger society.

HAS PARENTAL INVOLVEMENT MET YOUR GOALS?

1. *Are parents warmly welcomed and included in your classroom community?*

2. *Do parents understand how and what their children are learning and why the values of the caring classroom are important to their children's growth?*

3. *Are parents involved in home and classroom activities that value their own lives and experiences?*

4. *Do you give parents opportunities to see and hear some teaching and management strategies used in your classroom?*

5. *Do parents understand the guidelines of behavior in your classroom? Are they willing to support your efforts to help their children become more responsible and caring?*

Involving the Community

We have spent some time in prior chapters describing how teachers have included the wisdom and support of community members in various classroom activities. Do not forget their contributions at the close of the year.

Try These End-of-Year Activities

✼ ***Host an Assembly Program, Party, or Breakfast to Honor Your Supporters.*** In late May, Brenda and Sinclair, who created a partnership between Brenda's first graders and Sinclair's fourth graders, hosted a pizza party. They invited the community volunteers who helped them plant hundreds of flower bulbs in the fall. In late May, when the tulips were still in bloom, the students and adults toured the mini-gardens they created and finished in the cafeteria for a late lunch consisting of make-your-own pizza. The teachers knew the choice was a messy one, but they wanted the kids and the adults to interact. Instead of being served by the students, Sinclair's fourth graders wanted the adults to again create something with the students. They reasoned that it was a much better way to get reacquainted. Pizza creations became fanciful affairs, piled with cheese, vegetables, and sauce. Each guest became both a helper and an eater, and all left the party with a greater admiration and respect for the others.

✼ ***Volunteer your class to present a program*** for the town council or any other group organization, that has helped your students in the past. For example, second graders from a local school district presented their reader's theater version of Arnold Lobel's Fables to the local woman's business owners association. These were women whose understanding of and support for the work of the caring community could prove invaluable. The eight year olds were accomplished reader's theater presenters because it was a learning experience that involved them all year long. Their teacher, Allen Abby, had little to prepare. Other end-of-the-year activities took up most of his time and all of his energy! Once he arrived at the association's auditorium, he simply placed his students on stools in front of the audience and sat back to enjoy their carefully rendered versions of familiar stories and rhymes.

> *Ronald:* Poor Old Lady. She swallowed a fly,
>
> *William:* I don't know why she swallowed a fly,
>
> *Shelia:* Poor Old Lady, I think she'll die. . .

Organize an Adopt-a-Grandparent Program

First graders I know had been working with a group of senior citizens all year. In this adopt-a-grandparent program each six year old was matched with a senior who served as a warm lap, a compassionate ear, and an unconditional friend. At the end of the year, their teacher, Agnes Didden, wanted the children to honor the presence of these older citizens with very special gifts.

The children spent many class meetings discussing how they might create special surprises for their "grandparents." Every idea was rejected as not special enough. Troubled, Agnes turned to Carla Spector, the art teacher. Carla was invited to a meeting in which she presented the perfect solution. The children were delighted with the surprise and set about in groups to plan their presentation.

In early June the senior citizens arrived for the party. The first graders were dressed in their finest clothes. The room was decorated with signs and posters that said THANK YOU in many languages. There were balloons bobbing around the room with the name of each senior. Desks were pushed together to make a long table, which was filled with cakes and cookies the children and their parents made at home. Popcorn came from the kindergartners, who wanted to contribute something to this special day.

The first graders read original poems and stories that they created just for the afternoon. And just before the party ended, Lionel stood before the entire group. Lionel, the shyest of anyone in the class, could never have opened the program before he began working with his "grandparent," Mr. Calavetto. Mr. C. glowed with pride when Lionel began.

"Today we want to thank our grandparents for everything they did to help us all year. We thought and thought about what we could give you. And then Miss Spector gave us this great idea. She brought us all different kinds of beads and told us that each kind of bead stood for something special about a person, like courage and humor."

Touching Gifts

Erin continued. "She told us we could make special necklaces for our grandparents. First we had to decide what was special about each person. Mrs. Didden helped us write all the words." She held up a white card in which was written: COURAGE, HUMOR, STRENGTH, GOOD READER, FUN PERSON, and BEAUTIFUL WHITE HAIR. Then she held up the necklace she made with the beads that represented each of the characteristics. "This is for you, Mrs. Di Ginova. This is exactly what I think about you. Thank you for being my friend."

One by one, the rest of the first graders stood, read the list of characteristics they chose, and displayed the necklace to match. One by one, senior citizens rose to receive their gift and stooped to allow the child to place a necklace around his or her neck.

One by one, Agnes Didden handed out tissues to wipe away tears. She was entranced by her students and reminded—by their efforts to be kind—how the caring classroom had become a reality.

Connected learning is an important goal of a caring classroom. When your classroom moves into the community it offers to adults—many of whom have not been in schools for years—the opportunity to understand and support the values of kindness and concern, respect and responsibility. It is worth the time and effort to share with the greater community the intellectual achievements of our students as well as the social values they demonstrate.

Caring Classroom During the Summer

Some of your students may be programmed for every moment of their summer vacation. Others may have little to occupy them. Teachers who suggest summer activities and projects find that students are better able to remember the principles of the caring classroom they have worked so hard to build. Unless the idea of summer reinforcement is embraced school-wide, you do better to think about assigning work on a volunteer basis.

Here are suggestions for the summer enrichment:

1. *Contracts.* Students might write a contract for the summer in which they list activities and an implementation plan. (They might include reading, playing sports, helping around the house, learning something new). Parents should be asked to participate in such a contract which, by necessity, needs to be based on an honor system.

2. *Interviews.* Students could interview their local librarian to help them construct a personal summer reading list. Summer reading would extend the use of their literature response journals or their running records.

3. *Letters.* Design stationery that students could use to correspond with each other. Names and addresses could be entered in a schoolmade address book. Don't forget to include e-mail addresses as well.

4. *Postcards.* Preaddressed postcards, which have been decorated by students, could be sent to the teacher (at school or at home) in which students write to simply stay in touch.

Wishing You the Best

A caring classroom is a place where honesty and trust are more valued than retribution and punishment. Students are helped, through practice and reflection, to become respectful and responsible. I have shared my own experiences as well as the stories of other teachers with the hope that you will know that you are not alone in your quest. I hope that our stories will guide you as you continue your efforts to honor what it means to be a member of a caring community of learners.